THE BASTARDS

THE BASTARDS

Dirty Tricks and The Challenge to Europe

TERESA GORMAN
WITH
HEATHER KIRBY

A Pan Original
PAN BOOKS
in association with
SIDGWICK & JACKSON
LONDON, SYDNEY AND AUCKLAND

First published 1993 by Pan Books
a division of Pan Macmillan Publishers Limited
Cavaye Place London SW10 9PG
and Basingstoke

Associated companies throughout the world

ISBN 0 330 33511 1

1 3 5 7 9 8 6 4 2

A CIP catalogue record for this book is available from
the British Library

Typeset by CentraCet Limited, Cambridge

All speeches made in the House of Commons reproduced
courtesy of Hansard
Appendix listing Tory Rebel League reproduced
courtesy of the *Guardian*

CONTENTS

CHAPTER ONE
MARGARET'S DEMISE
*The Prime Minister is ousted because she resisted closer
ties with Europe.*

CHAPTER TWO
BEHIND THE SCENES
*The No Turning Back group and the Blue Chips are two
disparate sections battling for the soul of the party.*

CHAPTER THREE
NEW BOY
*The leadership battle between Major and Heseltine. I choose
Major because he is Margaret's man. Or is he?*

CHAPTER FOUR
THE BATTLE BEGINS
*Bill Cash, ardent anti-European, is ousted as chairman of the
important European Affairs committee.*

CONTENTS

CONTENTS

CONTENTS

CONTENTS

CONTENTS

HISTORY OF EVENTS

27 May 1993	Government reshuffle
14 July 1993	Lords vote on referendum
20 July 1993	Royal assent
22 July 1993	Social chapter debate. Government loses by 8 votes
23 July 1993	Vote of confidence: Government wins by 40 votes
23 July 1993	Prime Minister's 'bastards' remarks on TV
29 July 1993	Christchurch by-election
2 August 1993	Collapse of ERM

CAST LIST

ANTI MAASTRICHT

FRESH START

Rt Hon. John Biffen
Sir Richard Body
Nicholas Budgen
John Butcher
John Carlisle
Bill Cash
James Cran
Iain Duncan-Smith
Sir George Gardiner
Chris Gill
Teresa Gorman
Bernard Jenkin
Toby Jessel
Roger Knapman

Sir Ivan Lawrence
Barry Legg
Michael Lord
Tony Marlow
Richard Shepherd
Sir Trevor Skeet
Michael Spicer
Walter Sweeney
Sir Peter Tapsell
Sir Teddy Taylor
Bill Walker
John Wilkinson
Ann Winterton
Nicholas Winterton

MINISTERS – NO TURNING BACK GROUP

Michael Forsyth
Francis Maude
Michael Portillo
Edward Leigh

John Redwood
Peter Lilley
Neil Hamilton

LORDS

Lord Blake
Lord Harris

Lord Tebbit
Baroness Thatcher

LABOUR ANTI-MAASTRICHT

Rt Hon. Tony Benn

Dennis Skinner

PRO MAASTRICHT

Rt Hon. John Major *Prime Minister*
Rt Hon. Douglas Hurd *Foreign Secretary*
Rt Hon. Kenneth Clarke *Chancellor of the Exchequer*
Rt Hon. Michael Heseltine *President of the Board of Trade*
Rt Hon. Tristan Garel-Jones *ex-Deputy Chief Whip; Minister
in charge of Europe*
The Hon. Nicholas Soames *Minister for Food*
Rt Hon. Sir Norman Fowler *Chairman of the Conservative
Party*

WHIPS

Rt Hon. Richard Ryder *Chief Whip*
Irvine Patnick
Sydney Chapman
Robert Hughes
David Lightbown

AND OTHERS

Rt Hon. Tim Renton *ex Chief Whip*
Sir Marcus Fox *Chairman of Backbench 1922 Committee*
Betty Boothroyd *Speaker of the House*
Michael Carttiss
Rt Hon. Michael Howard *Home Secretary*
Rt Hon. Norman Lamont *Ex Chancellor*
Michael Morris *Deputy Speaker of the House*

ACKNOWLEDGEMENTS

This book was inspired by some off the record remarks made by the Prime Minister at the end of the Maastricht debate. It was written in three weeks between the closing of Parliament for the summer recess and going on my summer holidays. It is purely my recollection, not a definitive history.

I cannot vouch for the word-for-word accuracy of all the conversations I have reported but they all took place and I have not misrepresented what was said.

I dedicate this book to my colleagues who put their principles above their promotion prospects in a gallant attempt to keep political power in Westminster.

My thanks to Heather Kirby, who turned my fly-on-the-wall ramblings into a coherent text. To Brian Oxley who did the research and Jill Brown and Susanna Young for typing the manuscript. And to my husband Jim for putting up with me.

PREFACE

During the passage of the Maastricht Bill – the greatest threat to Britain's independence since the Second World War – over fifty backbench Conservative MPs felt strongly enough to vote against their government at some stage.

But they were only the tip of an iceberg.

There were probably a dozen more holding government jobs who could not vote without resigning and sacrificing their careers. In addition, another forty added their names to early-day motions critical of the Government, revealing a great deal of anxiety about further moves to integrate Britain with Europe.

Confronted with a politician apparently willing to sacrifice ambition for principle, many people are baffled. We were accused of being either publicity seekers or, as the Prime Minister described us, 'no hopers'.

And some of us had to battle with our constituency associations who thought we were disloyal to the party. But on an issue of this magnitude our instinct was to band together to save our democracy.

INTRODUCTION

'The Prime Minister's got the party by the goolies.'

The interviewer looked stunned but we were going out live so there was nothing he could do to stop me telling viewers how angry I was about what had happened in the House of Commons the previous night.

'At 10 p.m. we won a historic victory. By 10.30 John Major had snatched our triumph away from us by moving the goal posts. Unless we fall into line he is going to call a general election.

'He has given us two options: either we die by hanging or we have our throats cut. The choice is a Labour government or we will be dragged kicking and screaming into Europe.'

I was sitting in the GMTV studios on the morning after twenty-six Tories, who had fought for eighteen gruelling months against some of the dirtiest tricks ever seen in British politics to prevent the Government transferring our democracy from Westminster to Brussels, thought their battle was won.

The House of Commons had erupted with cries of, 'Resign!', 'Shame!' Triumphant cheers shook the rafters. But the Prime Minister stood up and announced that there would be a vote of confidence the following day, which meant that unless we fell into line, we would risk a Labour government.

Ever since Margaret Thatcher had been booted out of office in 1990, what had been a gradual slide into Europe had become an avalanche. The British people were to become, without their consent, citizens of a community with an alien type of government, which had never been explained to them.

1
MARGARET'S DEMISE

It was just coming up to eight o'clock as I left the breakfast television studios in the basement of Norman Shaw North, the old Scotland Yard building in Whitehall. A cold, drizzly morning matched my mood of anxiety and deep pessimism. Margaret Thatcher had the skids under her after failing to win the first ballot in a challenge to her premiership because, although she won far more votes than Michael Heseltine, she didn't get a big enough majority. It was two weeks since Tarzan had swung into action and now she was fighting for survival.

It was the umpteenth time I had been on television or radio in the last few days to defend her reputation. Apart from Cecil Parkinson and Norman Tebbit, the people in her Cabinet were 'unavailable' to the media. They were already distancing themselves from her, like rats deserting a sinking ship.

Margaret was not without blame for her difficulties. She was rarely seen in the tea room or around the bars of the House of Commons and had lost contact with her street-fighters on the back benches – a general must be seen by the troops before they go into battle. The community charge was worrying a lot of her natural supporters who thought it would kill their chances of re-election. Some, like Emma Nicholson, who knew her better than others, tried to warn her but the Prime Minister's reaction was high-handed: she told Emma to stop complaining and go out and sell the policy to her constituents.

'How can I do that when their community charge is going up from less than a hundred pounds a year to more than seven or eight hundred in many households?' Emma asked me over a cup of tea. Many other MPs with smaller majorities felt even more strongly.

'Why did she go to Paris before the first ballot knowing that her leadership would be challenged while she was away?' asked a colleague.

'It must be the only election contest in her political career she's not personally in charge of,' said another.

It was a sign of a loss of contact with reality that she seemed so distant from what was going on. Yet she knew the rules. They had been tested a year before when Sir Anthony Meyer was the stalking-horse who challenged her. She knew it required more than a simple majority to hold on to the leadership and that Michael Heseltine was snapping at her heels.

A significant number of people in her innermost circle had probably been waiting for their chance to see her off ever since the day, in 1975, when she first captured the leadership of the Conservative party. Geoffrey Howe for one.

But not all her enemies were in the Cabinet. Most people outside Parliament don't realize how influential the Whips are in advancing the careers of Members of Parliament. The 'right' people can be judiciously advanced up the greasy pole of promotion by the Whips. There were certain people in the Whips' office who did not share Margaret's scepticism over Europe and were only too happy to dance on her political grave. Nick Jones, BBC lobby correspondent, said he had never known the Whips to leak as they were doing: they wouldn't normally talk so openly to the likes of him but some were intent on spreading black propaganda, saying that Margaret couldn't survive a second ballot. Their blatant feeding of misinformation to journalists was an unprecedented breach of the secrecy which they usually maintain. I think it scandalous that a small minority should wreck the Whips' reputation for confidentiality.

But the Prime Minister's own judgement about the 'right' people let her down too. She was a snob about nobs. When choosing her parliamentary private secretaries, she plumped for people from the Establishment: Oxbridge and the aristocracy. Their role should have been to listen to the gossip, let her know what people were saying and to advise her of the mood of the House. Instead, they formed a phalanx of Praetorian Guards, haughty, superior, keeping backbenchers away from her.

You almost had to make an appointment to speak to her, even when she was walking through the division lobbies to vote. On the few occasions I sat at the same table with her in the tea room, I don't think she knew the difference between me and the tea-lady. To me, that didn't matter. What turned me on were her policies and her courage in implementing them. Under her leadership we had metamorphosed from a run-down old tanker into a fine fighting ship. She had transformed us into a country to be reckoned with.

I stood in the courtyard, wondering whether to go back to my office, which I shared with five others and where I would inevitably have to face someone, or whether to return to Lord North Street for a bit of breakfast with my husband Jim. Just then, Nicholas Bennett, a former minister who lost his seat in 1992, a stocky man who often teased me with chauvinistic remarks came hurrying across the courtyard. This morning he was obviously in no mood for idle banter.

'She's gone.' The stark statement stung me like a slap in the face.

'She can't have. I've just been on breakfast television, sticking up for her.'

'She decided to go at half past seven this morning,' said Nicholas.

'We have to stop her,' I said.

'We can't. She hasn't got enough support in the Cabinet. Too many of them have ratted on her.'

'Surely not Michael Portillo and Peter Lilley?' I said in amazement.

'No, not the No Turning Back people or Ken Baker. But most of the rest.'

The No Turning Back group were a loyal band of Thatcherite MPs and Nicholas, a combative, pugnacious character, was one of them.

'Some of the group went to see her late last night. They had to fight their way past Tim Renton [the Chief Whip]. They stayed for ages, trying to talk her out of her resignation, but I think her mind was already made up. They were almost in tears when they came back.'

The group had been having dinner together when a call had come from Michael Portillo, who was in Downing Street. He wanted some of them to come round urgently to talk to Margaret who was still considering what to do. Cabinet colleagues like Tim Renton and John Gummer were telling her that she could not win a second ballot; they were knocking down every argument her supporters put up. Neil Hamilton said he had never seen a more pathetic spectacle in his life as Margaret being attacked like that and not being in a position to defend herself.

'They went back again this morning at sixty thirty but Charles Powell refused them admission – they were told it was too early to see her. They waited around downstairs but by seven thirty she had already asked her private secretary to arrange an appointment with the Queen. She had decided to go. They couldn't save her.' It was this information that Nicholas was hurrying to convey to the breakfast news audience.

This story rang true. Last night I had been at a similar meeting of the '92 Committee, another group of Thatcher supporters, when we were interrupted at about seven o'clock. David Maclean, a bumptious Scot with a stentorian voice, burst in with an urgent message from Downing Street. Sir George Gardiner, chairman of the group, was wanted immediately in Downing Street to try to convince Margaret she still had enough support from the rank and file of the parliamentary party to win the second ballot. Later that evening we learned that he, too, had great difficulty in getting in to see her. There was no doubt that factions within the party, particularly the upper class Establishment, were trying to prevent her from finding out the extent of her support.

'It's terrible,' I said helplessly. 'Is there nothing we can do?'

'Nothing. She's gone. Now we have to act quickly to make sure we don't get landed with the wrong person. I'm going in to do some softening up.' And with that he disappeared into the studios.

As he walked away I stood paralysed by feelings of

despair, anger and total inadequacy. How could they do this to her after everything she had done for the country? Little did I know that the anger I felt then would soon be a drop in the ocean compared to the rage that was to engulf me when I watched as her betrayers tried to pressure me into selling Britain down the river.

I made my way out of the building and along Victoria Embankment, to the subway which leads beneath Westminster Bridge Road and into the Palace of Westminster.

I walked quickly. I wanted to get home to hear what was being said on television. In a daze I crossed New Palace Yard, where Margaret's friend Airey Neave had been murdered when his car was blown up by the IRA just before she became prime minister. It was almost deserted at that hour in the morning, except for the security men with their little mirrors on sticks, waiting to examine the underside of cars coming into the car park. I nodded briefly to the policeman at Members' Entrance and moved quickly through the members' cloakroom (which is just like the ones in an infants' school: we each have our own peg and we are still issued with a pink sash at the beginning of term – in which to place a sword – presumably for stabbing into opponents' backs).

As I passed a group of telephone boxes at the end of the gloomy corridor I stopped. I decided to phone Jim to tell him the news. As I pushed open the wooden door and stepped inside the phone box David Evans, who is as solid as a rock with a voice like a foghorn and a heart of gold, came round the corner.

'She's gone,' he said, his plump face sad and droopy.

'I know. It's terrible. What are we going to do?' David, a staunch Thatcher supporter, put his arms round me. That was too much. Suddenly I was sobbing uncontrollably.

'The bastards. They all owe their careers to her and now they've torn her down.'

'I know. I know. But she's gone now and we've got to think quickly about who will follow her.'

'I'm backing Heseltine,' said David.

I was taken aback. Heseltine had challenged her in the first ballot. I had him down as the arch villain of the piece.

'Heseltine! You can't possibly. Not after what he's done to her.'

'But he's our best performer. Look what a mess the economy's in. We need someone who knows how to run a business.'

I vehemently disagreed with his decision. 'I wouldn't vote for Heseltine if he was the last man alive,' I said. And I meant it. 'Margaret's supposed to support John Major but I hardly know him,' I said, the tears still running down my face. No doubt my mascara was smudged and my make-up looked a mess but at that moment I couldn't have cared less.

'Look, no one's been a bigger supporter of Margaret than me, Teresa, but we've got to have someone who can restore the morale of the party. Someone who understands the economy. Heseltine's the only one.'

'I expect they said all that about Hitler but I wouldn't vote for him either,' I said.

At that, David produced a large handkerchief and began to dab my cheeks. 'Do you want me to take you for a cup of tea?' he asked kindly.

'No. I'll stay here until I've calmed down and then I'm going home for some breakfast.'

I stood in the darkened telephone box taking gulps of air, sinking my teeth into my tongue, telling myself to stop being so stupid. Eventually, I dialled home and Jim answered.

'Margaret's resigned,' I said flatly. 'And I'm coming home for some breakfast. Put the kettle on, I feel like hell.'

My tears under control, I made my way across the vast expanse of Westminster Hall where members of the Royal Family lie in state and where Charles I was tried and condemned to death. Usually streaming with members of the public, it was cathedral quiet now and it struck me, as I thought about what I had just heard, that I could not have chosen a more appropriate place to be at this historic moment. My footsteps echoed click-clack, click-clack on the grey stone floor, and I concentrated on taking deep breaths to try to calm down, cursing myself for being so emotional. As I walked up the steps at the end of Westminster Hall I deliberately kept my eyes down to avoid the gaze of the policeman and guards manning the screening devices at St Stephen's Entrance. I got past them safely but as I began to descend the steps which led out to the street one of the policemen stopped me.

'Have you heard the news?' he asked. 'Is it true? Is the Prime Minister going?' He sounded shaken.

I nodded and looked up. The tears began to pour down my face once again. 'I can't walk out of here like this,' I said in exasperation.

'Why don't you come into our rest-room till you get a grip of yourself?' said the policeman, guiding me through the side door. 'Here. Have a bit of this chewing gum. That might help you.'

'You have some. You're crying too,' I said as two large tears rolled down his cheeks. 'The bastards,' I said.

'You're right. They're bastards,' said the policeman.

2

BEHIND THE
SCENES

In the parliamentary party there are a number of group-
ings; some for recreation, some for sport, some dining
clubs and others with the intent of capturing the
direction of the party.

Two such groups were the Blue Chips and the No
Turning Back. The Chips had been established longer; most
of their members were from Oxbridge; their politics were on
the left of the party; they believed in the Government being
involved in most aspects of people's lives. The NTBs, on the
other hand, were free-market Thatcherites. Most of the
members were from Scottish universities. They saw their role
as keeping the Thatcher government supplied with new ways
of reducing the activities of the state. Both groups were
hungry for power and when Margaret began to falter the
battle was on to choose a champion and get him or her into
the job. The irony was that both groups appeared to light on
the same man. Was that because nobody really knew him, or
was it because there was no one else? Both groups thought
John Major was 'their man' but one was mistaken. And one
of them, the No Turning Back group, turned out to be The
Bastards.

No Turning Back was the title of a pamphlet produced in
1985 by a group of thirteen MPs, ten of whom first entered
Parliament in 1983. They saw themselves unashamedly as a
ginger group to support the radical instincts of Margaret

Thatcher. They were worried about the cautious souls in the party who thought that enough had been done and that the Government should lie back and rest on its laurels. The British people, they said, never re-elected governments burned out of ideas.

The pamphlet was a clarion call to extend the freedom of choice already enjoyed by a minority. State schools should be made independent and should be run by a board of parents and staff, they said. All new private sector housing should be freed from rent control and security of tenure. Students should be given loans, not grants. People should be encouraged to take out private medical insurance by making the premiums tax deductible. And Britain should retain its independence from Europe.

Some unkind souls called the group 'Margaret's Kindergarten' and its members certainly had a head start in government! Nicholas Bennett, an Englishman with a seat in Wales who entered Parliament with me in 1987, became a junior minister in the Welsh office. Michael Forsyth, Francis Maude, Eric Forth and Angela Rumbold were already in the Government. By 1990 John Redwood, Peter Lilley and Michael Portillo were all tipped for Cabinet jobs, later becoming 'The Bastards' about whom John Major complained. It was pretty certain that all were sceptical of government policy to join up with Europe, and particularly of the Maastricht treaty. Edward Leigh, one of the joint authors of *No Turning Back*, later a junior minister in the Department of Trade and Industry, was eventually sacked by John Major for expressing his scepticism about the Maastricht treaty.

The original group of thirteen MPs expanded rapidly and continued to meet regularly at the offices of the Institute of Economic Affairs in Great Peter Street, a stone's throw from the House of Commons. (And, incidentally, within spitting distance of Tory Central Office.) Under the guidance of Ralph Harris, later Lord Harris of High Cross, they published a number of pamphlets which had considerable influence on government policies. This was the same Ralph Harris who, in the 1970s and 1980s, had had such a profound influence on Margaret Thatcher and several key players in her early Cabinet. Both he and they were to play an important role behind the scenes in our battle to defeat Maastricht.

Publicly, the NTB people had to stick to the party line and, in Parliament, they kept their distance from the Eurosceptics. But in the tea rooms, at private dinners and in the bars, they made it clear they shared our sentiments.

The Blue Chip group was formed in 1979 when five new Conservative MPs found themselves sharing an office in Dean's Yard, behind Westminster Abbey. They were William Waldegrave, Chris Patten, John Patten, Tristan Garel-Jones and Richard Needham. It was Needham, you may recall, who in 1990 when he was a minister in the Northern Ireland Office, was overheard on his car telephone describing Margaret as 'the old cow'.

The Blue Chips were friends, they were gregarious and they were out of sympathy with Thatcherism. They met two or three times each term at Tristan's house in Catherine Place where his Spanish wife, Catali, cooked for them. One of the most popular, but least conspicuous, members of the group was John Major.

The Blue Chip had not been their idea for a name. It was coined by the Whips, who were amused by the number of earls, marquesses and old Etonians involved, but the group's members were happy with it just as Margaret Thatcher rather liked to be called the Iron Lady.

During the early part of the Thatcher government, with three million unemployed, the Blue Chips published a pamphlet called *Changing Gear*. In it they attacked economic dogma – their code meaning Margaret's policies – and called for more government investment in industry at a time when the Government was pulling back. To cynics on the right of the party it looked suspiciously like a return to the old days of Harold Macmillan and Harold Wilson. And Blue Chip was very much in favour of European integration.

John Major did not become a regular member of the group until after *Changing Gear* was published so he could not be tarred with all its views, although presumably he must have shared them. In any case, the pamphlet was vague on detail but strong on nostalgia: the time before Margaret Thatcher came to power. Tristan Garel-Jones was firmly rooted in the Whips' office; it didn't seem to harm anyone's career prospects. Chris Patten was marked down as their choice for the future leadership of the party, but he wasn't in a position to make a bid at the time Margaret was ousted: he had a marginal seat in Bath and the chances were that he would lose at the next election which, of course, is what happened.

Those members of the group who were not promoted while Margaret was prime minister were rapidly drawn into office when John Major took over. William Waldegrave and Chris Patten were already in the Cabinet when John became prime minister and when Chris lost his seat in 1992 he was sent to govern Hong Kong. Richard Needham and Tristan Garel-Jones became junior ministers. Ian Lang was made Secretary of State for Scotland and Peter Fraser, now a peer, was brought back into the Government as Lang's deputy. Sir Nicholas Lyell became Attorney General while Robert Atkins became Minister of State for Northern Ireland. Alastair Goodlad, a late member, went to the Foreign Office and Nicholas Soames became Minister for Food. Even Lord Cranborne, who was not an MP nor, at the time, a member of the House of Lords, was brought into the Government by the antique device called a Writ in Acceleration. Who knows why the Prime Minister went to such lengths to get his old pals into government? There must have been plenty of people who could have done the jobs. But it tells us something about the Prime Minister's determination to have as many of his close chums around as possible. To judge from their publications, his premiership was more likely to be marked by the policy style of Edward Heath than by Margaret's 1980s' zeal. The Thatcherites in the parliamentary party somehow overlooked this when they decided to back him for the leadership.

In his ten years in Parliament, he showed no interest in Thatcherite groups like the '92 or the No Turning Back, and he must have been privy to some of the scheming that went on against Margaret among the Blue Chips.

John Major's 'nice guy' mask slipped slightly on the day that the Maastricht Bill completed its committee stage. Addressing a dinner of Conservatives, he described the Eurosceptics as 'defeatists who make your flesh creep. They practise a sort of phantom grandeur, a clanking of unusable suits of armour but they are running against the tide, a tide that will flow ever more strongly into the enlarged community.'

So there we have it. Powerful – and vitriolic – stuff. And we were to get more in the same vein after the last battle was fought.

3

NEW BOY

Everyone has his or her own view on what caused Margaret's demise, but no one disputes that Europe played a large part in it. There were many Euro-fans among Conservative MPs and Margaret's scepticism did not go down well with them. Once she was out of the way, they believed Parliament could go on to the next stage of the United Kingdom's integration into Europe without any significant opposition.

In the bitter aftermath of her resignation on Thursday 22 November, we sceptics had assumed that John Major shared Margaret's reservations on Europe. Indeed, when running for the leadership, he had assured the '92 group, another band of Thatcher sympathizers, he was the biggest Euro-doubter of them all.

Looking back, we should have realized. It was he, along with Douglas Hurd, the Foreign Secretary, who had persuaded Margaret to take Britain into the Exchange Rate Mechanism, something she had strongly resisted while Nigel Lawson was Chancellor. Despite her reservations, Lawson had begun the process back in 1987 by shadowing the Deutschmark. This caused the high interest rates, up to 15 per cent, which were responsible for the growing number of bankruptcies, mortgage failures and job losses in the country.

I was very concerned about the difficulties I was hearing about at that time from people in my constituency. These were decent, hard-working, middle-England people who had never asked for anything in their lives. They were coming to me, very distressed, asking if I could help them to get a council house because their lovely detached homes had been taken back. They were people who had responded to Margaret Thatcher's enterprise philosophy. They had expanded their businesses, built new factories and suddenly, because of rocketing interest rates and a drop in orders, could not cope. They hadn't done anything wrong, they were completely blameless, and instead of being angry they were often apologetic. I would have been livid and I was angry on their behalf.

It was an open secret that Margaret Thatcher's resistance to the pro-European policy of her Foreign Secretary and Chancellor helped to generate the bitter attacks which Lawson and Sir Geoffrey Howe made on her after they resigned from the Cabinet, body blows from which she never fully recovered. Margaret's enemies within the parliamentary party were fairly well known – Lawson and Howe certainly made their positions very clear. But what of John Major? He had risen so fast, becoming Foreign Secretary after only ten years as an MP and Chancellor soon afterwards; she clearly thought he shared her views or she would not have gone out of her way to groom him to succeed her. This patronage recommended him to people, like me, on the right of the party, who believed that he would take a tougher, closer Thatcher line on Europe than the other candidates.

But were we mistaken? And how reluctant was he to come forward as a candidate? How much of his campaign was planned well in advance? The journalist Alan Watkins says in his book *A Conservative Coup* that John Major had been preparing himself for succession for four years. Even before the first ballot, while Margaret was still away in Paris, a piece appeared in *The Times* by the then political editor, Robin Oakley, who is now with the BBC. John Major was emerging as a contender if Margaret Thatcher decided to stand down, it said. He would present a fresh and more youthful image, with his technical grasp and winning manner. I do not believe such articles appear by chance: they are the result of carefully orchestrated conversations made on 'lobby terms' in which the person planting the idea is not named. John Major was obviously seen, by those with the power to pull strings, as the man to stop Heseltine.

Perhaps the desire to stop Heseltine getting the job blurred our perception of the degree to which John Major shared Margaret's views on Europe. Although his policies as Chancellor had established him as economically dry, committed to controlling spending, he had been the man to take us into the ERM. He had a bee in his bonnet about a common currency which he called 'the hard écu'.

Between the first and second leadership ballots, enough of her Cabinet colleagues had told Margaret that they would resign if she continued as leader, to make her throw in the towel. Meetings were taking place all over Westminster: in tea rooms, the corridors, the library, the committee rooms, and, no doubt, in the numerous gentlemen's lavatories dotted around the Palace of Westminster, where, it was rumoured, careers could be won and lost.

John's team was swiftly in action, a group of well-organized supporters headed by Norman Lamont, then Chief Secretary to the Treasury, Michael Howard, then Employment secretary, John Gummer, then Agriculture minister, Peter Lilley, who was Trade secretary at the time, and Norman Tebbit, all, except Gummer, reckoned to be on the right of the party. The team settled into a tiny cottage in Gayfere Street owned by Alan Duncan, now MP for Rutland and Melton but then a businessman, where they established their campaign headquarters. The garden backed on to my own.

I went down to my constituency in Billericay to see the chairman of my association and to find out the views of the party workers there. They supported John Major by a large majority. On the day after the first ballot another article had appeared in *The Times*, which said that although he was dry on the economy he was soft on social issues. 'I am a free marketeer, but beyond that I believe in treating issues on their merit,' he was quoted as saying. In the opinion of *The Times*, 'The formula is hardly brave and certainly not visionary.'

Differences over entry to the Exchange Rate Mechanism and the European monetary system had led to Nigel Lawson's departure from the Cabinet, but if there was a single event which set off the challenge to Margaret's leadership it was her incautious remarks made in the Commons that she did not think the hard écu promoted by the Chancellor would become widely used. Her outburst certainly did not endear her to the ministers on the Treasury bench: it was a signal that she belonged with the hard-line Euro-sceptics.

One afternoon as I drove back to my home in Lord North Street, I saw Norman Lamont, John's campaign organizer, leaving the headquarters looking chipper.

'I hear you're in charge of the campaign,' I called out to him. 'How's it going? I'd like to have a word with John sometime.'

'I'm sure he'd love to see you. Especially if you're going to support him. He's seeing people over in the Commons. Give James Arbuthnot a ring. He's arranging visits,' said Norman, with a wave and a smile. Although I didn't know Norman personally, I knew a bit about him from his saucy press coverage, and he always crinkled his eyes at me endearingly. I liked him. We have too many grey men in parliament.

I also realized that I knew very little about John Major, which wasn't surprising. In politics, where so much is going on, you really only get to know people if you serve on a committee with them, or if they happen to share your views and prejudices. I had hardly spoken to him except on odd occasions when he passed the time of day with me in a friendly way whenever he came across me sitting in the tea room or the library. He seemed a warm person. He's very nice to everyone, I thought, but behind that façade there's obviously an ambitious and determined man.

As a new MP, I often used to sit alone in the library, which overlooks the Thames. It is one of the finest libraries in the country; the walls are lined with books which overflow into the corridors and you can get back numbers of almost any political journal you care to name. It has deep green-leather armchairs designed for sleeping in, and they are so huge I have to perch on the edge otherwise my legs dangle in mid-air. I've often been in there during a late sitting when the windows have reverberated to the sound of snoring.

In the early days I'd sit in there wondering what on earth I was doing in the House of Commons. There is no organization in the party for inducting new members into Parliament's little ways. It's a bit like joining a school then being left to decide what classes you should be attending. Some of the new intake seemed to buzz around purposefully, always in a hurry to get somewhere. I later realized they were the ones who had worked as research assistants or in some other job around the House before getting elected. They knew the ropes – or appeared to. I didn't like to ask them what they were up to. And I didn't like to ask the old hands, all of whom seemed so busily preoccupied. They might have thought I was twopence short of a shilling. So when John stopped for a few words and asked me how I was getting on, it made a very good impression.

I took up Norman's suggestion and called James, a studious young man with an aloof manner, and later that day made my way behind the Speaker's chair, to the Holy of Holies where ministers have their rooms. They were designed by Pugin and are very Victorian with deep maroon and green patterned wallpaper, sort of William Morris type. John Major's room was modest in size and had a window overlooking New Palace Yard, at the front of the building. He had a huge, solid oak desk, and paintings of former chancellors stared down on us.

Looking back, it is a safe bet to assume he was never one of us. In fact, on 23 November, *The Times* commented that 'most Tory backbenchers regard Mr Major as the most Thatcherite of the three contenders, although it is something of a mystery why he should have acquired this reputation'. During subsequent debates on Maastricht he grew closer and closer to the position of Edward Heath, who had waited all these years to get his revenge on Margaret. Once, in a policy speech to the Conservative Group for Europe at the Inter-Continental Hotel, John went out of his way to pay Heath a lavish compliment for taking Britain into Europe. Little by little he openly distanced himself from the views of the right while keeping up the rhetoric that he was the 'biggest sceptic of them all'. But at the time of the leadership contest we were lulled into thinking he was our man. We were completely self-deluded, partly because he was Margaret

Thatcher's choice and partly because we considered him the best bet to beat Heseltine.

Douglas Hurd had at first been thought to be the main contender if Margaret failed the first ballot, with John Major consistently declining to rule himself out of the running and equally refusing to commit himself if she didn't win an outright victory. While all the speculation was going on in London, he had disappeared to his home in Huntingdon to recuperate from an operation for an infected wisdom tooth.

As I was ushered into his room on the ministerial corridor, I commiserated with him: 'How are you feeling after your operation?' I asked solicitously. Many regarded it as a very propitious toothache: it meant he had contrived to be away from the furore so could be viewed as a man with clean hands. He certainly had no intention of being a man with no ear to the ground, though, because Jeffrey Archer was summoned from his home in nearby Grantchester, outside Cambridge, to report on what was happening in the capital.

'It's nice of you to come and see me, Teresa, and thank you, I'm fine now,' he answered, and came straight to the point. 'Are the right wing going to support me?'

I said, 'Yes, but what I would like to know is, what are you going to do for small businesses? Are you going to keep Europe at arm's length? Because the regulations pouring out of the EC are driving them mad.'

He smiled and nodded but didn't give any commitment. So I launched into my next favourite issue. 'You must put some women in your Cabinet,' I told him.

I felt a little in the way as people came in and out carrying large brown envelopes marked 'Very Urgent' which they placed purposefully in front of him. Clearly, standing for election as prime minister didn't stop him from running the Treasury.

'I know about your interests in women. But I'm not in a position to promise tax relief on child care,' he replied. (This was a subject I had raised with him on more than one occasion, trying to get him to include it in his budget.)

'No, no. I've not come about that. The women in the country are grieving for Margaret. I don't want them to think we are the male chauvinist party,' I said earnestly. 'Some of our colleagues round the House are openly boasting that they're only too pleased to have got rid of her.'

I could have added that most of these people were numbered among the dedicated Euro-fans and even included some who, hours before, had enjoyed the status of being in her inner circle. It made me feel sick.

'I do understand what you're saying, Teresa.' He looked away from me at several of the packages which had been placed in front of him and I got the message. This wasn't the time to put my point across. 'Why don't I ring Norma? She's over at number eleven. I'm sure she'd love to see you for coffee. Would you like to go?'

I was dumbfounded but realized he was trying to get me out of the room without hurting my feelings.

'Thank you, I'll do that,' I said.

'I'll give her a call and tell her you're coming,' he said, and picked up the phone.

I went over immediately to No. 11 Downing Street for coffee and Norma insisted I stay for lunch. 'I have some frozen roasted chicken joints and can make a salad,' she said. 'The trouble with living in official residences is you never have any proper food at either house. I try to buy stuff and leave meals ready in the fridge for John but he usually gets

23

home late and is too tired to want to eat anything.' We talked about how she felt about becoming the wife of the Prime Minister – and what she should wear if John won the ballot.

The battle for the leadership was hotting up, the election was only two days away and I was appearing on radio and television supporting Margaret's man, John Major.

I saw Heseltine as the main threat to the policies she had introduced. His track record was that of an interventionist who liked spending large sums of public money to make a big, showy splash: Docklands, Liverpool, Westland, where he could turn up to engineer some favourable publicity. I didn't dislike him personally. I hardly knew him except by his performances at the dispatch box or at party conferences, where he was a real pro. I just thought his political schemes a colossal waste of public money. I went everywhere sporting my Stop Heseltine badge. It had arrived in my office from I know not where. I was aware that the TV cameras would focus on it and it would give an extra twist to my remarks.

On my way to and from my office in Norman Shaw North I had to pass the room of Michael Mates, who was orchestrating Heseltine's campaign. The door seemed always to be open with Mates inside on the telephone, sweet-talking people into supporting his candidate.

Michael Brown, a member of the No Turning Back group who ended up voting for Heseltine, came up with his own solution to the endless telephone enquiries about who he was going to support. He recorded this message: 'If you're a reporter, I've nothing to say. If you're a candidate for the leadership, I'd like to be the governor of the Cayman Islands. Now, please leave your message.'

Michael Brown also had his own way of finding out which of the candidates was likely to suit him. He telephoned them all. 'Can I have a brief meeting with you?' he asked.

He got to see all three and said to each, 'Here I am, a humble backbencher, and I am interviewing you for this job. What are you going to offer to win the support of this right-winger?'

Wonderful stuff.

I bumped into my friend David Evans in the members' tea room one evening.

'I hope you've changed your mind about supporting Heseltine,' I said to him.

'No, I haven't, Teresa, I still think he's the best bet. I think the Tory party are going to be bloody annoyed about what we're doing to Margaret and we need a big character to fill the gap.'

Later, as I walked along the back corridor, I bumped into Margaret's parliamentary private secretary, Peter Morrison. 'How's Margaret?' I asked.

'Bearing up. She's come to terms with it and she's doing all she can to get John elected, phoning people. If you know anyone who wants to talk to her let me know.'

'I know some people she ought to talk to. Have you heard that Michael Brown and Edward Leigh, both Margaret men, are thinking of supporting Heseltine? And David Evans says he's going to. But I think he's reluctant. A personal word from Margaret might swing him round.'

'I'll have a word with her,' said Peter. 'Thanks for the tip.'

Next day I saw David. 'Did you hear from Margaret?' I asked.

'Yes, I did. I went to see her in her room behind the Speaker's chair. It was heartbreaking. I feel like kicking them all in the teeth, the ones who've done this to her. She spoke to me for twenty minutes and asked me for her sake to support John Major.'

'And what did you say?'

'I told her that I didn't think I'd be able to. She said she was very disappointed and she'd like me to sleep on it.'

When the news came through that John had won the leadership election, I felt a sense of relief. I came down from the committee corridor where the election had been held and joined some colleagues in the members' smoking room — actually a bar — for a drink. The room was full of little groups: some Heseltine or Hurd supporters looking glum and sipping whisky, while John's supporters talked loudly, looking happy and drinking champagne.

Nicholas Soames came through the door. He moved quickly round the room leaning forward to each group, saying something rapidly. At last he reached our group as we stood in the corner by the bar. 'Michael's on his way to the bar,' he said nervously, looking directly at me. 'I hope you're not going to be nasty to him, Teresa,' staring at my Stop Heseltine badge. Nicholas is enormous, over six feet tall and as wide as a barn door. He reminded me of a huge spaniel that could pick me up by my neck and give me a good shaking. I think at that moment he would have liked to do just that.

'Why should I be? We've just won and he's just lost. I shall be magnanimous to him in defeat. Anyway, why would he care what I think? I don't think he's ever exchanged a word with me since I came into this place.'

Nicholas scuttled off towards the door, his yellow socks peeping out above his Gucci loafers.

The other members of the group turned towards me. 'You're not going to bite Hezza's head off, are you, Teresa?' they said, laughing.

'The idea of him being the least bit nervous of me is laughable,' I said.

Just then, he came through the door surrounded by a group of camp followers, his head in the ozone layer. Gently, they steered him round the room where he stopped to have a chat with each group.

'Well done.'

'A good clean fight.'

'You did well.'

'Excellently.'

From the comments you would have thought he had just won the election.

As he approached our group, the conversation dried up.

'You put up a good fight, Michael. Will you have a glass of champagne with us?' asked one of my companions. I turned and looked up in his direction. He glanced down at me and half nodded. I took a deep breath. 'No hard feelings, Michael. It's back to work now,' I said.

So, on 28 November, Mr Nice Guy John Major had won the leadership vote and become prime minister. Margaret left Downing Street, in tears, having earlier made one of her final soundbites.

'It's a funny old world,' she said.

If she felt any bitterness, she didn't show it. But I was

furious at the way she had been treated, and so were most women. Even Germaine Greer, the strident left-wing feminist, wrote a touching article about her in the *Daily Mail*, mourning her passing from the premiership. Funnily enough, she made an issue of the fact that Margaret had served the nation in the way that mothers serve their families. And today when ministers want to disown a policy, they pretend it was foisted on them by 'Mother'. It's a disparaging reference that makes their mostly male civil servants chuckle.

Germaine also wrote, 'The bitter truth is that it is probably harder now for a woman to head a British political party than it was before. Margaret Thatcher put on such a hard act to follow. The men in grey suits will not make the same mistake again . . . much to the loss of every woman in this country.'

John soon announced his Cabinet. There were no women in it.

'Are you disappointed there are no women in the Cabinet?' asked the television reporter when the list of names were announced.

'I am,' I replied.

'What are you going to do about it?'

'I'm going to squat on the front bench,' I said. That remark attracted a lot of flak from many Tory women members of the parliamentary party who were trotted out to denounce me. In politics sycophancy is considered a much greater virtue than honesty.

4

THE BATTLE BEGINS

T hose of us who thought Margaret's demise would be the end of the purge of Euro-sceptics were mistaken. They had succeeded in getting rid of her, now they began to target the rest of us.

On 13 November 1991, Bill Cash was standing for re-election to the chairmanship of the backbench Committee on European Affairs. Standing for other offices were Christopher Gill, James Cran and Tony Favell, all Euro-sceptics. Tony Favell, a large, jolly man, friendly and patriotic to a fault, had resigned as John Major's parliamentary private secretary soon after the then Chancellor took us into the ERM as he had disagreed so much with that policy.

Backbench committees are often used like a supporters' club by the Government in the hope that the members will come into the chamber and give three cheers to the Secretary of State when he is propounding Cabinet policy. But if you disagree with a government policy, it is a good position from which to bowl a few googlies at its wicket – and be noticed by the media, who always relish an internal battle. Bill Cash had used it for several years to great effect. To the media he was Mr Anti-Maastricht.

The committee chairmen are re-elected at the opening of each parliamentary session. It is strictly a backbenchers' event: the Government and the Whips, by tradition, keep their noses out of it. If you seriously want to be elected to one of these committees you must rally your own chums to come and vote for you; on this occasion Bill Cash could rely on the support of all the members of the '92 dining club with its ninety or more members. Various clubs on the right and on the left of the party vie with each other to claim the chairmanships of these committees.

In the week before the election, rumours started to circulate that Sir Norman Fowler intended to challenge Bill Cash. This in itself was unusual: ex-government ministers don't usually attempt to become chairmen of backbench committees because they have already had their go at fame and glory. Norman has been a faithful party servant for as long as anyone can remember. He held a number of ministerial jobs in Margaret Thatcher's Cabinet before parting company with her in January 1990 'to spend more time with his family', as the saying goes. Now a backbencher, he was, strictly speaking, eligible to stand. When asked by the media he consistently denied that this was his intention. But at the eleventh hour he changed his mind or, as we suspected, his mind was changed for him. The Government would have been very pleased indeed if Bill were no longer able to pass on his thoughts to the nation wearing the hat of chairman of the Committee on European Affairs. (It was not the first, or the last, time the Government has intervened to influence the chairmanship of backbench committees: Nicholas Winterton was ousted from his position as chairman of the Select Committee on Health after bringing out a critical report of the Government's reforms of the health service.)

Tension was running high. That morning I received a letter in the internal post to remind me to turn up at 6 p.m. to vote for Bill and the rest of the slate. So just before six I made my way through the committee corridor on the first floor of the House where the election was to be held. As soon as I got within hailing distance I could see something unusual was going on. The corridor was completely blocked with a milling crowd of MPs and lobby correspondents, who are allowed to congregate in the vicinity of the room on these occasions to learn how the voting has gone as soon as the winners are declared. This particular committee meeting was hot news and they were there in force.

I joined the jostling crowd trying to force their way in through the door. Voting begins strictly on the hour and lasts for five minutes. The committee rooms are light and airy with huge windows overlooking the Thames but they have terrible acoustics. The high ceilings are festooned with black microphones hung on fine wires so that the Hansard writers who produce the House records can hear every word. Like the ministers' rooms, these walls are also adorned with richly patterned Victorian-style wallpaper in gold and maroon and huge paintings of long-forgotten battles and Members of Parliament. (I have yet to find a portrait of a woman politician anywhere in the House of Commons beyond the basement. A portrait of Lady Astor, the first woman to take her seat in the House, is hung on a wall in a basement corridor immediately opposite the men's lavatories.)

In some of the smaller committee rooms the seating is arranged in a semicircle but in the large ones like this, room 14, the seating is set out as it is in the chamber, two sides facing each other. Instead of benches, there are narrow oak desk tops, complete with ink wells. The committee chairman and officials sit on a dais at one end and down the middle is a long table where all the papers are put. The voting papers are issued at random by the Whips to anyone who sticks his or her hand out. The whole business is quite disorganized but since usually very few members turn up for these elections it works quite well.

This time, however, more than 250 MPs were fighting to get in. People were jostled and some were nearly knocked over as everyone struggled for ballot papers. Some had managed to grab several and were passing them back through the crowd. As far as I could tell, just inside the door a phalanx of pro-Europeans were blocking the entry of the latecomers. Those of us near the door stretched our hands forward like refugees pleading for a piece of bread. I realized I was not going to get into the door by normal means so, being on the small side – I'm only five foot two – I turned sideways and began to insinuate my narrowest edge between the heaving hips and thighs. As I neared the front of this mass the Whip's voice rose above the noise: 'Voting is closed! Close the doors!'

'Close them? Most of us haven't even been able to get in,' shouted somebody at the back.

'It's a fix,' said someone else. Suddenly Norman Tebbit appeared above the crush, standing on the heavy oak table in the middle, in an attempt to bring some order to the chaos. This was, to put it mildly, most unusual parliamentary behaviour.

'Many MPs have not yet got a ballot paper. Everyone who was inside the room by five past is entitled to a vote,' he shouted. Tempers were running very high and I half anticipated a punch-up. Now, as I reached the front of the crush, I could see there was room inside for all of us if only the doors had not been blocked. I spotted Bill Cash, a worried look on his face, and Norman Fowler, attempting not to look too smug. Even more surprising, there were Sir Edward

Heath and Sir Geoffrey Howe. Party grandees of their status rarely turn up to these events and their presence indicated just how thorough the whipping had been by Norman Fowler's campaign manager, Bob Hughes, eager beaver and new boy. Hughes had entered Parliament at the same time as me, voluntarily became assistant to Edward Heath and was an out and out Euro-fanatic.

'This is a disgrace. It's a fix. Someone has organized this.' They certainly had – but the comments and pleas fell on deaf ears. The Whips were not going to issue any more ballot papers. I didn't get one myself.

From somewhere within the room the organizers of the vote were now collecting the papers. Two more ballots had to be held for the vice-chairman and the secretary. This time I was able to grab two lots of papers by putting out both my hands.

Immediately behind me another colleague shouted: 'There will be an official complaint about the way this election is being conducted. We expect this behaviour from the Labour party but not from Conservatives,' he declared. 'It's not cricket!'

To console him I turned round and handed him my spare ballot paper. 'Quick, fill that in and do your grumbling later or you'll miss the next vote, too,' I said.

When the votes were declared it was a complete rout for the Euro-sceptics. Norman had replaced Bill as chairman and candidates favourable to the Government's position on Europe took over as vice-chair and secretary.

Christopher Gill, the MP for Ludlow and a former councillor who owns a chain of pork butchers in the mid-lands, and James Cran, MP for Beverley, a Scot and a former northern director of the CBI, were both businessmen and, like me, didn't really fit into the influential parliamentary networks. They were furious not so much at losing control of the committee but by being outsmarted by the Government and the Whips in what should have been a backbench affair. Now the Government was in a position to control statements given out, demonstrating backbench support for its European policies. This strategy was meant to suggest to people outside Parliament that there was almost universal approval within the parliamentary party – which was far from the truth.

James and Christopher made their way down to Central Lobby to find a quiet spot where they could talk without being overheard.

'Well, that was a bloody disgrace. We can't let them get away with it. The Government's determined to wipe out all criticism of its European policies when you and I know that a third of the parliamentary party is distinctly uneasy about them,' said James, when they were seated in the corner. 'Just look at the number of people who turned up to vote. This is a big issue in the party and I'm not going to stand by and let them ride roughshod over us. I think we had better talk to some more colleagues. We'll have to get our act together in a much more organized way if we are to have any impact on government thinking.'

It was out of this conversation and the disgraceful events in the corridor upstairs that the group who became known as the Fresh Start group of Euro-sceptics, or Euro-realists as we preferred to be called, grew. Christopher and James became its organizers and unofficial Whips, inviting other colleagues known for their opposition to the Government's European policy to join. At first they arranged informal meetings in one of the committee rooms off Westminster

Hall until it became too small to accommodate the numbers who turned up. These included John Biffen, a former Leader of the House, Sir Rhodes Boyson, Michael Spicer and John Butcher, all former ministers. Other regulars were Sir Richard Body, Sir Ivan Lawrence, Sir George Gardiner, Nicholas Budgen, Bill Cash, Toby Jessel, John Carlisle, Michael Lord, Tony Marlow, Sir Trevor Skeet, Sir Teddy Taylor, Nicholas and Ann Winterton, John Wilkinson, Richard Shepherd, Bill Walker and Roger Knapman. And from the new intake of MPs elected in 1992, Barry Legg, Bernard Jenkin, Iain Duncan-Smith and Walter Sweeney. All of them could be described loosely as from the right of the party but by no means all were Thatcherites. From the left came Sir Peter Tapsell, who would not normally find himself in such company. On this issue, however, he found himself in complete accord.

These were not the only colleagues who attended our meetings from time to time and voted against legislation to lead us deeper into Europe. In addition there were those who, during the long-drawn-out debates on the Maastricht Bill, voted against the Government on points which were particularly disagreeable to them. In all, over fifty Conservative backbenchers felt, at some time, unable to support their own leaders.

5

NOT ONE
OF US

In April 1992, the Prime Minister decided to take a chance and go to the country in a general election. Norman Fowler, the new chairman of the backbench Committee on European Affairs, was John Major's minder during the campaign, making sure the Prime Minister's soap box went everywhere with him. The election was a long shot: the economy was still faltering; unemployment was rising and many sections of the Tories' natural supporters were living through bad times. The main issue was the economy, not Maastricht. All the main political parties were agreed on Maastricht; only the Ulster Unionists spelled out their opposition to it. And a few Euro-sceptics in the Tory party made no secret of how they felt. I put in my election address that I wanted 'a Britain united and independent'.

Our luck was in. Labour went into the election promising an increase in taxes, a crass and elementary mistake. No one wins elections by promising to take more money off the voters if they should be daft enough to put you in power. Our parliamentary majority was slashed from a healthy 100 to a – by comparison – fairly feeble twenty. If the truth be told, John Major and the rest of us were relieved to achieve even that result. It was a workable majority, or so the Prime Minister thought. The debates on the Maastricht treaty would prove otherwise. With a majority of 100 a rebellion would have been futile. But with twenty, a group of determined backbenchers can change government policies. The Government can no longer allow itself the luxury of doing just as it likes.

Five months before the election, on 10 December 1991, John Major left Britain to attend the Maastricht conference to negotiate the next stage in European integration, even though Europe was increasingly viewed with suspicion by the British public. But before he went, a debate took place which etched itself into the memory of millions who watched it. Not because of the excellence of the oratory – God forbid, we get few enough instances of that – nor because of any headline-grabbing antics from members – we get too many of those – but because Margaret Thatcher made a speech.

It was poignant and painful to watch her looking awkward in her new position on the back benches where she had not set foot for 30 years. She was sitting at the end of the third row to the left-hand side of the Prime Minister and looking down at the front bench where she had sat as prime minister for so long. Now John Major occupied the place. Next to him sat Norman Lamont, his Chancellor, and Tristan Garel-Jones, one of his closest associates and a dyed-in-the-wool Euro-fanatic. Like the lowly rest of us, Margaret had a good view of their bald patches and Brylcreem.

John Major had given Garel-Jones the job of piloting the Maastricht treaty through the Commons. Sitting opposite them was Neil Kinnock then still Leader of the Opposition and the man who had done more than anyone to turn the Labour party through a 180° turn from an anti- to a pro-European party. In 1972 Kinnock voted against going into Europe. Now, if you closed your eyes and ignored the Welsh accent, it was difficult to tell the difference between his views and those of the Prime Minister. John Major spoke first and then Neil Kinnock. As soon as he sat down Margaret rose to speak.

Dressed in one of her favourite suits, dark blue with white edging around the collar and revers, she looked uncharacteristically nervous. I could have sworn that her hand, clutching some prompt cards, trembled slightly. I was sitting near her, willing her on.

'The fundamental issue that will confront the Government at Maastricht is that the draft treaties propose an enormous – and to me an unacceptable – transfer of responsibility from this House, which is clearly accountable to the British people, to the European Community and its institutions which are not accountable to the British people. Our authority comes from the ballot box and we are talking about the rights of the British people to govern themselves under their own laws made by their own Parliament. It is the character of the people which determines the institutions which govern them and not the institutions which give people their character. It is about being British and about what we feel for our country, our Parliament, our traditions and our liberties. Because of that history, that feeling is perhaps stronger here than anywhere else in Europe.'

The House was packed. Everyone was listening intently. Only Frank Haynes, a Labour member and an old adversary, famous for his booming voice and his down-to-earth comments, rose persistently, trying to interrupt her. Eventually he succeeded.

'For old times' sake, I will give way to the Honourable Gentleman before I go on,' she said.

Now was Frank's chance to get it off his chest. 'Just a year ago the Conservative party committed a dastardly act against the Right Honourable Lady. I have missed her from the dispatch box ever since. If she were still in the seat of power what would she be negotiating at Maastricht?'

'I am making a pretty good fist of explaining that right now,' said Margaret to laughter. She was beginning to get into her stride. I felt relieved. The eyes of those on the front bench were fixed, they stared ahead as if trying to catch a glimpse of some Utopia, hovering just above the benches opposite.

'Anyone who does not consider a referendum is necessary must explain how the voice of the people shall be heard. We should not deprive the people of their say on rights which we are taking away not only from them but from future generations. I understand that my Right Honourable Friend the Prime Minister wishes to keep his options open and that a referendum may not be popular with some members of my party, but I doubt whether they have thought it through.' Here she went on to explain why the circumstances of Maastricht demanded that a referendum be considered, and then continued, 'We should not make a massive transfer of power to the Community which is not accountable to our electorate.' She sat down to a chorus of 'Hear, hears' from the Euro-sceptics but stony silence from the front bench.

The speech was strong, forcefully delivered and, as usual, commanded the attention of the House. I spotted no friendly faces turned towards her from the front bench but there were plenty of kind words from supporters around her on the back benches.

So long as Margaret remained in the Commons her presence would haunt those who had usurped her. My advice to her would have been to stay just where she was: she was still a powerful force. But in June 1992 Margaret took the short walk to the Lords. Perhaps she did it out of kindness to the new Prime Minister. Or perhaps because she found it frustrating, or humiliating, after all those years in the driving seat. When the Bill was sent to the Lords for consideration, there she was waiting to grab the steering wheel again, along with seasoned fellow travellers Norman Tebbit, Cecil Parkinson and many old friends.

After the election, a group of Euro-rebels in the Commons, led by Michael Spicer, ex-minister, began to meet regularly to discuss growing concern about the implications of Maastricht. At one of our regular meetings we discussed whether to share our anxieties with the Lords. The treaty would eventually go to their House when the Commons had finished with it. Many active members of the Lords, whether for or against the Maastricht treaty, believed that people should have their say through a referendum. The Government, of course, was implacably opposed. Toby Jessel took on the job of co-ordinating these activities. He regularly reported which of their lordships were willing to participate in a group similar to ours in order to maximize their efforts. In the Lords they would be dealing with a different audience, with different priorities but with a stronger feeling about the importance of the independence of the country. We decided to invite their lordships to a dinner, which was held at the St Ermin's Hotel.

It seemed strange on that evening to be sitting with a new set of conspirators some of whom were completely unknown to me. They tend to introduce themselves by their titles not their names. 'Devonshire', they say, not 'The Duke of Devonshire', or 'Donnington', not 'Lord Bruce of Donnington'. I suppose this avoids telling you whether they are mere lords and not viscounts or dukes. There were a couple of dukes there that night.

We went round the table giving our personal impressions of the key points worth raising in debate until we hit on an issue which seemed to excite their lordships. This came when one of my colleagues began to draw comparisons between Maastricht and the last war: the similarity between fighting for our liberty in 1939 and again in 1992 struck the right note. Their lordships were visibly fired up: we knew then that we had a bunch of willing helpers.

In Parliament John Major's return from the Maastricht conference was presented as 'a triumph'. In his speech to the Commons he boasted that he had refused to accept the social chapter which would impose enormously expensive burdens on employers. He had also refused to agree to the requirement to move to full financial integration. This seemed to indicate to some sceptics that John Major's heart was, after all, in the right place. His speech was greeted with much waving of order papers on the Tory benches as a sign of approval and support. Jonathan Aitken, a prominent Euro-sceptic whose London house has hosted many meetings critical of the European Community, made a speech praising John Major for his negotiating skills. He was soon rewarded with his first government job in eighteen years, as a junior defence minister. I don't think many people begrudged it to him, although there were a few wry smiles. But other Euro-sceptics, myself among them, remained deeply suspicious of the direction in which the Prime Minister was leading the country over Europe and particularly his dedication to the Exchange Rate Mechanism, which was causing so much misery.

6

CARLTON CLUB CONSPIRACY

The 1992 general election had given the Prime Minister a new authority over Parliament and the country but there were considerable misgivings among those of us who disliked the prospect of closer political union with Europe.

In the members' lobby, tea rooms and bars, animated discussions took place between pro- and anti- MPs. People were sounding each other out as they munched their way through beans on toast, crumpets and slices of the tea room's famous carrot cake. It is mostly over food, and occasionally a drink, that you gauge the spectrum of feelings about an issue and find out who are your likely allies.

One day early in May, I left the tea room and made my way to Central Lobby: this is the part of the House the public sees, the principal floor, and is arranged in a series of chambers, one leading to another through short, picture-lined corridors. The enormously high, octagonal lobby is like the foyer of some grand railway station with people milling about all the time. Sometimes, when an organized lobby takes place, it is so packed that you can't get through. In the morning, streams of schoolchildren walk past in crocodiles on their first visit to Parliament. At other times it is almost deserted except for our regular tramp who sits all day on one of the benches always smiling at the policeman who guards the entrance which leads into the members' lobby and through which no one else is allowed to pass without permission.

While I was sitting on the green leather benches in the corner just outside the door which leads to the Whips' inner sanctum, I spotted Christopher Gill, the member for Ludlow, and James Cran from Beverley. As they were both former officers of the backbench Committee on European Affairs, I thought it would be interesting to get their views. 'I've just been talking to George Gardiner and he seems to think the treaty offers us a pretty good deal,' was my opening remark.

Christopher and James exchanged glances. 'Well, it does sound all right until you get into the small print,' said Christopher cautiously.

'The social chapter stuff is pretty horrendous. But even if we don't take it on board officially it's unlikely our partners will let us get away with it. They'll find some other way of imposing it on us. Look how they've managed to get round the forty-eight-hour week.' This was a reference to a directive of the European Community which sought to put a maximum on working hours. The Government objected but the European Community used other means to impose it on us. A forty-eight-hour week sounds innocuous enough to most people but in fact it was a mandate for employees and trade unions to demand high extra payments for 'unsociable' working hours. The French, sticklers for their special interest groups, gained an opt-out for their bakers to enable their employers to insist on an early start in the morning to ensure that the French passion for fresh baguette was not under threat. Anything else would have had a devastating effect on their way of life and that was not how the French viewed the European Community.

'We know that most of this European legislation isn't what it seems to be. James and I have strong misgivings,' said Christopher.

Bill Cash had similar views. Although ousted as chairman of the European Affairs committee, he was still a formidable Euro-opponent. A constitutional lawyer and one of the best informed people in Parliament on Europe, his public statements were a constant thorn in the flesh of the Government.

'I am thinking of organizing a dinner at the Carlton Club for a few of us who have misgivings,' said Christopher. 'Just a chance to talk things over. Would you be interested in joining us? We might be able to organize some opposition during the second reading of the Bill.' It's a joke in Parliament that whenever two people meet together to hatch a plot one of them is bound to be a Whip's nark and it wasn't long before the lobby correspondents were on to this event. When gossip is fresh and hot a member strolling through the lobby will be approached by anything from one to half a dozen lobby correspondents who enquire politely whether you will be attending the rumoured event.

On such occasions I usually deny all knowledge, although I know that someone must have spilt the beans. By 12 May it was pretty obvious that the press were on the trail and were going to make this into a news event. Anything which smells even slightly of rebellion is ideal fodder for their programmes and columns. So when four of us arrived at the Carlton Club by taxi we weren't surprised to see television cameras outside. You get an idea of how Elizabeth Taylor or the Princess of Wales feels when you have to battle your way through a group of reporters and photographers while flash bulbs go off in your face. It's quite exciting.

Of all the gentlemen's clubs in London's Pall Mall, the

Carlton is the most conservative. Women are not yet admitted so when Margaret became prime minister, they had to make her an honorary man in order to grant her membership. So identified is it with the Conservative party that the IRA has targeted it in one of its infamous bombing attacks on London. As a woman, I find most of these London clubs rather dreary places with elderly, somnolent staff who look as if they have retired there from the stately home business.

As we climbed the stairs to the first floor, portraits of former Conservative prime ministers glowered down at us but there was no sign of Margaret Thatcher. In the dining room several members were already assembled drinking a glass of wine.

'What are we going to do about the press outside?' asked Bill Cash. 'They're all slavering for a quote.'

'I think we shouldn't say anything,' said Roger Knapman.

'We can't say *nothing*. Nick Budgen has already agreed to do a spot for the ten o'clock news. What we have to decide is what we want him to say.'

'You're not suggesting that any of us can control what Nick says?' I asked.

'No, you certainly cannot, my dear, although I am always interested to know what you think I ought to say,' said Nick, tongue in cheek. A barrister and professional wordsmith, Nick is a master of the gentle putdown.

'Perhaps Bill Cash should do it – he was the chairman on European Affairs,' said someone else.

'I don't want to stop Bill doing anything he feels like but I have committed myself to do something and the television people are waiting outside so I shall keep my word. But you don't have to worry about me, I shall not be telling them we're hatching a plot up here,' said Nick to general laughter.

We were all in high spirits and as I looked round the table at the twenty or so people present I saw one or two surprising faces. It turned out later that at least one of these reported back to the Whips on what took place over dinner. In fact, all that happened was that each person gave his or her point of view; Ann Winterton was the only other woman present. Although some of our dinner guests were never seen again at our gatherings, this meeting proved to be the first of many among the Fresh Start group, as it came to be known when it merged with Michael Spicer's dining club of Euro-sceptics.

Any attempt to keep the Carlton Club dinner low key was dispelled when it was splashed on the late television news and in next morning's newspapers. There were photographs of a bunch of us stepping out of a taxi or sidling in or out of the club.

From now on we were marked men and women.

7

MAASTRICHT MACHINATIONS

A prime minister can sign a treaty but before it can come into effect Parliament has to approve it. The Maastricht treaty required us to amend the legislation which had brought the European Community into being: the treaty of Rome. To do so the Government introduced a Bill to the House of Commons called the European Communities (Amendment) Bill, colloquially known as the Maastricht Bill. It was this which was battled over for eighteen months. At the first reading of a Bill the title is read to the House of Commons, which means the Government simply announces it, which puts it on the map. Soon after, it is given a second reading and the contents are debated, usually for a day or two. At the end of the debate if the House votes 'aye' the Bill goes to a committee for detailed examination.

Members of Parliament are summoned to attend votes by a 'whip', a timetable sent to MPs each Friday with details of the work of the House for the next week. Compulsory debates are underlined three times. Hence the expression three-line-whip, a term related to hunting: the whipping in of the hounds. The Maastricht Bill was definitely a three-liner. Those of us who, from time to time, voted against the Government on a three-liner were often accused of voting with Labour, but I don't recall a single occasion when it was pointed out that Conservatives supporting the government position found themselves with some rather dodgy bed-fellows. On most of those occasions the Labour party and the Liberal Democrats voted with the Government – except for votes on the social chapter. To my mind it should have been very uncomfortable for good Conservatives to find themselves tucked up with their political opponents.

Some of us, however, were taken pretty severely to task for daring to stick with our principles. Poor Liam Fox and Alan Duncan, newcomers to the House, were lambasted by one columnist, who predicted they would be 'incarcerated on the back benches' and, despite their abilities, would never be allowed near a job in government. James Cran was thrown off the Trade and Industry select committee for expressing his anti-Maastricht views. 'And it was made known to me that I had a high chance of getting on to a delegation on a two-week visit to (wait for it) St Helena and the Falklands! Remember who spent some time on the former . . .!' The implication being that he would get anywhere only if he toed the line. Hints and nods of this sort were to become the Whips' stock-in-trade as they tried to pull our strings. And for many MPs, the ones who spend their lives swanning around on delegations, such a tactic would work. They'd be broken-hearted to be put on a Swanee black list. But since St Helena happens to be where Napoleon was exiled to and were he was left to die, perhaps it's just as well that James consistently ruled himself out. James said later this had been the worst year of his life.

Maastricht, and most of the Euro-legislation which had gone before it, is essentially socialist in nature, designed to create a centralized structure for Europe controlling every nuance of labour relations, industrial and commercial life, with lots of interventionist policies and, of course, huge subsidies. I was amazed that so many of my Conservative colleagues could go along with it.

The Maastricht Bill received its second reading on 20 and 21 May and the vote revealed for the first time the size of Tory misgivings. Twenty-two Conservative backbenchers rebelled against it, including me. Another four abstained, making a significant number in view of the Government's overall majority of only 20. An even larger number of Labour rebels voted against, although some of them did so not because they opposed the treaty but because they objected to the exclusion of the social chapter: they wanted it warts and all. But the Government was not under any real threat because they could rely on the official Labour party and the Liberal Democrats who both wanted the treaty to be ratified. The majority was more than enough to give John Major a peaceful night's sleep.

(Incidentally, to the casual visitor Maastricht is a pleasant, sleepy, provincial Dutch town but to anyone with a sense of history its name should have rung alarm bells. Guy Fawkes, an artillery officer in Philip of Spain's army, was based there when, with his co-conspirators, he hatched the Gunpowder Plot. In the First World War Hitler was hospitalized there and used the time to draft *Mein Kampf*. It also boasts the first discovery of dinosaur bones.

In 1990 the heads of governments in the European Community met there for a political conference which was to give birth to a dinosaur of a treaty, wedded to the past, destined to blow the British parliamentary system apart and possibly lead to civil disobedience.)

But the Prime Minister's peace was about to be shattered. On 2 June 1992, our Danish partners in Europe held their first referendum, as required under the Danish constitution.

By a small majority, but a majority nevertheless, the Danish people rejected Maastricht. Without the agreement of all twelve partners in the EC the treaty could not be implemented. This was a bombshell for the Government but a bonus for those who had misgivings. The members' tea room was buzzing with excitement. Soundbites were rehearsed for the debate on the following day. I met Christopher Gill in the members' lobby.

'The Danes have saved our bacon,' he said.

By the evening this was already a cliché. Gossip and ideas spread through the House like greased lightning. That afternoon I could hardly wait for the statement promised by the Prime Minister which would give us a chance to air our support for the Danes. In the course of the day I remember speaking to Tony Marlow and Nicholas Winterton, suggesting that after Douglas Hurd's statement we should try to call for three cheers for the Danes. No doubt other harmless but enormously pleasurable plots were being hatched. Then I spotted Peter Shore, a long-standing opponent of Europe. I rushed over to him and flung my arms around him. 'Isn't it wonderful, Peter?' I said, hugging him.

If he was shocked by my sudden embrace he was too much of a gentleman to show it.

'The Vikings have returned again to save our country,' he said quietly, with a broad grin on his face. He is a thoroughly nice man although, like a soldier home from a long war, his body language expresses the demeanour of a disillusioned man who has lived a long time with disappointment.

His obvious enthusiasm for the result boosted my own high spirits. I felt an enormous sense of relief. The action of the Danes would not only scupper the treaty but would save me the job of battling against the official party line, never a comfortable position to be in. Everyone likes to be loved!

'Great news,' I whispered next day as I squeezed past rows of knees to the seat I had reserved for the Prime Minister's statement. If some of the older hands found my enthusiasm a trifle naïve they did not show it. Even Euro-fanatics like Ian Taylor, who looks as if he has eaten too many good dinners and is pomposity incarnate, managed a watery grin.

The Danes had derailed the Government's timetable for the treaty. John Major decided to postpone the committee stage of the Bill to give himself time to consult with the other eleven members of the EC. And he needed further backing from Parliament before going on to the next stage. His tactics were to have a day's debate to gain approval and pave the way for the committee stage at which the details could be picked over line by line.

8

FRESH START
IS BORN

The Danish referendum was a terrific morale booster. Teddy Taylor, an indomitable anti-European, tabled a motion, congratulating the Danes while others of us signed letters of congratulation, which were sent out to leaders of the 'No' campaign in Denmark. Bill Cash, with his seemingly endless contacts, frequently travelled over there in the run-up to the referendum to reassure the Danes of support in Britain for their point of view. So, too, did Sir Richard Body, the MP for the rural constituency of Holland with Boston. Over six feet tall, his upright bearing belies his seven decades; he is one of the House patricians, an excellent speaker and a natural gentleman. A former chairman of the Select Committee on Agriculture, he hated the Common Agricultural Policy which he saw as the ruination not just of British farming but of the British countryside. On his visit to Denmark he spoke to a different audience from Bill; he tended to travel backwards and forwards with people who had a distinctly green tinge to their politics. Several others of our group also made the pilgrimage. Among them was Michael Spicer, the mild-mannered former government minister and close associate of Margaret Thatcher.

I was not surprised that on the day after the Danish referendum Michael was buzzing around the Members' lobby, an early-day-motion form in his hand. 'I want you to sign this EDM on Maastricht,' he said. 'It calls on the Government to rethink its whole Maastricht policy.' There is a kind of routine on these EDMs: you tend to sign those of people you like and trust even if you don't always entirely agree with them. It's a form of camaraderie in the House which binds people to you so that when you want some support they feel they owe you one back.

Most are composed by backbenchers so that they can send them on to their local newspapers just to let them know that their MP is still alive and kicking up about something worrying a handful of constituents. Most are destined for the dustbins of history. Occasionally an EDM attracts enough signatures for it to become of interest to the lobby correspondents, the Whips' office and even those most insular of individuals, the secretaries of state.

This one of Michael's was special. Ninety-one Conservative backbenchers signed up, which in itself was remarkable: ninety-one is almost a third of all Conservative MPs. But, even more significant, the figure represented almost two-thirds of all backbenchers. It did not include junior and senior ministers, all of the Whips and those ministerial lackeys known as parliamentary private secretaries, who, by tradition, are not allowed to sign an EDM.

Michael's EDM called on the Government to postpone Maastricht and make a fresh start. It was a clarion call, later uniting those of us who wanted to oppose further integration with Europe.

Michael's EDM appeared in the Order Paper next day. Its long list of supporters was the number one topic at the Whips' meeting held at No. 12 Downing Street, the official residence of the Chief Whip, Richard Ryder. 'We have a serious problem on our hands,' said Richard, 'and I want action.'

A close friend of the Prime Minister, Richard is a boyish-looking man and is part of the East Anglian mafia even though he had also been a close associate of Margaret's, working in her office in Downing Street for several years. His wife also worked as one of Margaret's private secretaries. 'You must all have a word with your charges and get them to withdraw their names,' he instructed his team of Whips bluntly.

The next day's Order Paper bore the fruits of the Whips' efforts: several MPs had been nobbled. The way the Whips set about picking off anyone who dared to challenge them on the referendum issue, dirty tricks and all, became both a legend and a blot on the way in which this wonderful country of ours is governed. Hartley Booth, Margaret's successor in Finchley, and Lady Olga Maitland, from Sutton and Cheam, were among the first to change their minds. David Evans, the jovial Cockney member for Welwyn and Hatfield, a self-made millionaire and former owner of Luton Football Club, had added his name to show he was on our side, which was very brave of him, but had to withdraw because he was a parliamentary private secretary. Michael Shersby from Uxbridge, who represents the Police Federation in Parliament, also had second thoughts, and, most surprisingly of all, James Hill, member for Southampton Test. James had been a Euro-fanatic for as long as anyone could remember and he must have signed the EDM by mistake!

Michael Spicer's triumph, his inside knowledge of government, and his pleasant nature, marked him out as an acceptable leader of our dissident group, which took its name from the Fresh Start mentioned in his EDM. Initially regarded by the Whips as a sort of Dad's Army of misfits, we soon formed as disciplined a task-force as any SAS brigade. Our membership and our meetings were hot topics in the Whips' office. I remember peering in there on some errand and being startled to see the complete list of miscreants printed out on a large billboard, no doubt the better to remind them of whom they had to pick off.

There are fourteen Tory Whips. Members are divided up into groups by geographical area and one Whip is given responsibility for each area. They are like school prefects. Their role is not to try to change our opinion, but to convince us that the Government's policy is more important than our principles. They must get to know their charges. They see that you toe the party line and they give you a wigging if you miss a vote or, heaven forbid, vote against the Government or abstain. You are expected to tell your Whip in advance if you intend to commit this sin. All sorts of pressure is applied. Failure to inform the Whip brings a sharp note in the post next day, demanding an explanation. On a three-line whip, even the dying are brought in to vote.

Whip: 'Dear Teresa, I noted you were absent for the three o'clock vote [that's three o'clock in the morning]. This is a serious offence. Explain please.'

Me: 'My dear Sydney. At two o'clock in the morning I went home and fell asleep on the sofa. Unfortunately my division bell was out of action, please forgive me.'

People who feel strongly enough to vote consistently against a particular policy are given a severe warning. Their constituency association chairman might be informed – informally, of course. They may be taken off a favourite committee or dropped from an official trip abroad. The ultimate sanction is to have the whip withdrawn, after which, technically, you are no longer part of the parliamentary party.

This punishment is not viewed lightly by your constituency association and may lead to them disowning you at the next election. MPs are sent to Parliament to do their best to represent their constituents and to use their own judgement. They are supposedly free to be as independent as they will, but the party system is designed to turn them into obedient servants. Parliament is run like a cross between a gentlemen's club and a boys' public school, with the Whips as school prefects. The way to get on, if you don't happen to come from the right school or the right family, is to be a bit of a toady and never step out of line. This accounts for the often dull quality of the front bench in contrast to the colourful iconoclasts on the back benches. There is precious little room in party politics, except in a crisis, for a visionary or independent spirit.

We had everything to lose. By resisting the Government on a policy so dear to the Prime Minister's heart, we were sacrificing all chances of promotion under the present regime. Some were even threatened with de-selection. Adultery is a more acceptable sin than defying the party Whips. Behind a smokescreen of principled rhetoric most MPs are shallow and self-seeking and it is rare in the history of Parliament to find a group, knowing the risks, who are willing to set themselves on a potentially self-destructive political course.

During the passage of the Maastricht Bill, the group hovered at around twenty-six stalwarts. Some of their constituency associations considered them brave, others treacherous. Each individual was left to battle for his or her own survival. But we banded together to save our democracy from being submerged in Brussels.

The Danish referendum and the debate that followed gave added impetus to our group and our regular meetings were well attended. We soon had too many members to fit comfortably into the small committee rooms off Westminster Hall and now met regularly in room J on the lower ministerial corridor inside the House of Commons. This became known as the bunker. It amused us to think that three floors above us ministers were plotting their strategy on the Maastricht treaty, while here, in our windowless and airless dungeon, we plotted how to undermine it.

To be effective in the chamber, we needed to set up contacts with key people in other parties to find out what they were up to. Roger Knapman, the member for Stroud and a chartered surveyor, was roped in to set up lines of communication with the Ulster Unionists and other fringe groups such as the Welsh Nationalists and Scottish Nationalists to see if they would vote with us. Christopher Gill and James Cran covered the Liberal Democrat and Labour parties.

The genial Michael Spicer chaired the meetings with a relaxed and amiable manner but with all the skills necessary to silence a windbag. At each meeting we would assess our chances of victory. This always depended on our intelligence sources supplied by our unofficial whips because we were a tiny group compared with the 650 MPs, the majority of whom would vote for the treaty. This was the official policy of all three main parties. Only the Ulster Unionists were against. Once or twice during the committee stage we succeeded in getting the Government to back off from a vote. Michael would be detailed to negotiate it with Chief Whip Richard Ryder. Our goal was to secure the promise from the Government of a referendum.

I was thoroughly enjoying myself; it was the first time I had joined a group of male colleagues who shared a common interest. Mixing socially with your colleagues in the company of the family is commonplace but since the wives usually organize these occasions women MPs are rarely invited. At least, I was not! Now, suddenly, I was invited to meet my colleagues' wives who seemed genuinely delighted to see me. To a woman they supported us up to the hilt.

I received invitations to speak in other group members' constituencies and I began to develop a veritable fan club as their female members reported favourably on my performance. For the first time since entering Parliament I began to appreciate the meaning of being one of the boys.

No one had asked me to do a serious job, apart from organizing ten-minute-rule Bills, since I had entered the House. Now, during crucial Maastricht debates, when members had to be around all evening I had to chase them even into the dining room. The tradition is that you join any table where there is a vacancy, regardless of whether you know, like, or share the opinions of the people who are already there. It is an interesting system and one way in which you get to know people. When I spotted one of our group I would make my way to the table and whisper my report in his ear.

'What are you up to, Teresa? Undermining the party? Causing the Whips problems? Trying to stop history? Or making a date?' Quips came from all sides but the nearer the

individual was to being a Euro-fanatic, the more sarcastic
their tongue. They were all intrigued to know what we were
up to.

'Could you come back to the chamber?' I whispered and
grown men, many of them former ministers, responded to
my requests like lambs instantly and unquestioningly.

We took it for granted that the Whips probably had a
plant among our supporters. None of us knew who it was
although each of us had our own suspicions. The Whips
had built up a legend around themselves about knowing
everything that went on in the Palace of Westminster, and
even more about the private lives of Conservative members.
I have often wondered why, if this is to be believed, they
didn't tip off those of our colleagues who were making an
absolute ass of themselves, before the press got hold of the
story.

More important than worrying about what the Whips
were getting up to was keeping our group's deliberations
from the lobby correspondents and in this, I think, we were
successful. As individuals we were as different as the contents
of a bag of liquorice allsorts and some of us were inclined to
gossip more than others. But for the most part discipline was
pretty good. Michael constantly reminded us of the importance of confidentiality. Although we held a wide variety of
views and came from the right, left and centre of the party,
we were all able to unite around one policy: the call for a
national referendum on the Maastricht treaty. We believed
that by taking the issue to the public, we would not only
engage their interest, we could also unite public opinion
behind us. Time and again this was raised by one of us in the
chamber and time and again the Prime Minister resisted the

idea. It was part of our plan to try to force the Government to incorporate the need for a referendum into the Bill during the committee stage.

Among the regular attenders at our meetings were four of the new intake of MPs. There had been five but John Whittingdale, no doubt after being leaned on, dropped out. The only test of membership, voting against the treaty, was too much for some. The four who remained formed a little sub-group of their own, working through the material of the treaty to bring out points of particular interest to them and in the course of time they published a book in which they expressed their views called *Maastricht: Game, Set and Match?* Those who failed to remain true to the cause drifted away. We did not witness their departure. We merely noted their absence. We older hands had a particular admiration for the new boys who stuck with us. These new Members were prepared to put their principles before their prospects of promotion – something quite rare in politicians. A new MP who becomes involved in a group which the Government and Whips view with disapproval is probably sacrificing his or her chances of promotion in the short term, and may find themselves on the back benches for the rest of their days. There were plenty of examples: for instance, Teddy Taylor had to resign his job as a minister in the Scottish Office in the 1970s for opposing government policy on Europe. A great politician and parliamentarian, he has consequently spent twenty years in the wilderness. The only way to escape this fate is to do a complete U-turn and publicly confess your mistake, for which you can usually expect to be rewarded with some minor government post.

When we set out I don't think any of us anticipated the

bitterness and bullying we would encounter. Nor did we realize how much we would need to stick together, physically for our own protection and mentally to support each other in the face of unparalleled pressure.

9

END OF TERM

Before the Parliamentary recess began at the end of July the Euro-sceptics decided on an end-of-term social dinner, this time at Rodin's restaurant, on the corner of Great Peter Street near the Houses of Parliament. It's nice to get out of the House to eat because it can become very oppressive, but we have to choose somewhere within sound of the division bell in case we are needed to vote. The restaurant occupies the central atrium of one of the majestic buildings which line Millbank, facing the Thames. It is partly occupied by the BBC and ITV. It is patronized by MPs, the media and lobbyists.

The atrium itself is magnificent, eight storeys high with a glass roof. Although you are inside, you feel as if you are outside. It has real trees and little tables covered with bright red tablecloths, and feels like an outdoor café or French bistro. The food is French and excellent, a change from the canteens in the Commons.

Although we were eating in a private dining room, we had to cross the big open space and it was impossible for us not to be noticed by half the journalists there. We saw them dive immediately for their walkie-talkies to alert the news desks.

Twenty-six people turned up but not the same twenty-six who had been at the Carlton Club. Throughout the eighteen months of our campaign the magic number of twenty-six cropped up time and again but membership was fluid; the individuals varied as some lost their nerve about opposing the Government while others found their resolve strengthened. Resisting both the blandishments and the bullying of the Whips takes a certain type of mettle. It was amusing to see them come and go. In the early days John Townend, Andrew Hunter and Rhodes Boyson turned up to dine; later they were replaced with some of the new MPs who joined the House of Commons at the 1992 election.

The club, for such it seemed to us regulars, consisted of a hard core of about fifteen. By the time the first half dozen of us arrived, television cameras had appeared outside the door and filmed us coming in. Waiters scuttled in and out bearing fresh bread and the next course. Each time the door was opened a camera was shoved in too until, in the end, Bill Cash agreed to go outside and give them a piece to camera. That would usually satisfy them.

'Those vultures out there can hear every bloody word you're saying in here,' said John Carlisle, arriving late for the meal. 'Why doesn't someone kick them out?'

'Why don't you do it, John? You're the one with a reputation as a bruiser.'

'Me? I wouldn't soil my hands on them,' said John, in his usual arch manner.

All politicians have a love-hate relationship with the press. And it works both ways. Without them, we wouldn't be able to advertise our activities to our constituents, but when they try to stick their cameras into a private meeting, that is entirely another matter. On this occasion, however, I think their presence gave our meeting a certain frisson – a feeling of importance.

Talk at dinner ranged over a number of topics: the problems of the economy, the Government's intransigence over the ERM, the need for a referendum on the treaty, and we rehearsed a possible strategy for the committee stage. As ever, Bill Cash knew the legislation in great detail and would have taken up all the evening explaining it to us in the minutest of detail if his appetite had not intervened. Teddy Taylor, with his long history of opposing Euro-legislation, waxed as gloomy as ever on the Common Agricultural Policy while John Biffen and Sir Peter Tapsell contributed quality and gravitas on parliamentary procedure and the financial implications of the single currency. The trouble with politicians is that once they start speaking it's almost impossible to stop them and Michael Spicer was too nice to cut across the point which anyone was making – even if we had already heard it from the previous three speakers. Round the table we went; everyone had to have their say, however tedious. Toleration was laying the groundwork for the comradeship we would need in the following months as pressure from the Whips built up.

When Parliament goes into recess each year for the long summer break I imagine the British public heaves a sigh of relief – those of them, that is, who take a blind bit of notice of what goes on in Parliament. Most punters in the saloon bar and in the Conservative clubs round the country can be relied on to complain about the 'bloody long holidays which you MPs get'. But without the recesses, a good many of us would go quietly mad. The post, of course, continues to arrive but that is mainly dealt with by our secretaries. And it is surprising to see how the flow of urgent matters from constituents seems to take a summer break as well. But for MPs who are required to stay up half the night debating legislation, which often the country could well do without, the recess provides a much-needed break from Westminster. Members can spend more time with their families, who are usually stuck in the constituency while Father or Mother runs the country. On returning home members are quite likely to find that the children have grown three inches, the dog has died, mother-in-law has moved in and the wife or husband has run off with the tennis coach. Some members, hyped up on media coverage of their activities in the House, report extreme withdrawal symptoms. They tend to book foreign holidays in countries where CNN news bulletins can be picked up, and let their office know they are available on the end of a telephone in the Bahamas lest an opportunity for a 'down-the-line' interview should crop up. Secretaries of state are supposed to stagger their holidays with their junior ministers but don't always achieve it. Hence, when some unexpected national crisis arises, they are often caught in a remote village in Sardinia on the side of a mountain with one telephone box and a crackly line.

Such is the quality of the British civil service that most crises are arranged for September when the Prime Minister is back in Downing Street and his senior colleagues are once again behind their desks in Whitehall. I always find it heartening that the country can function perfectly well for three whole months, August, September and October without Parliament.

Makes you think, doesn't it?

September 1992 found me and five colleagues in Australia on an official delegation to the Commonwealth Parliamentary Association. The purpose of such a visit is to cement international relationships and to show the flag. Our visit was considered opportune because the Aussies' prime minister, John Keating, had recently upset the Queen by giving her a bit of a cuddle. Our kindred down-under obviously did not know what every one of us takes in with our mother's milk: the Queen may dub a commoner on the shoulder but a commoner may not touch the royal body. It is this sort of hiccup that goodwill visits like ours are designed to smooth over.

'I hear you were on television – again,' said Alan Howarth, the leader of our delegation. 'What were you talking about this time?'

'Not politics,' I hastened to assure him. I was anxious for Alan to understand that I was not usurping his position as spokesman for our group. 'Just women's things. I was talking about hormone replacement therapy. You know, that stuff I'm always going on about in the Commons. It's what keeps me going when all you young chaps are asleep in the library chairs.'

'Well, I'm glad they didn't ask you about the Queen and Mr Keating,' he said. I'm sure he had prepared a little speech in case they invited him to give his comments and would have been quite put out if I had got in first.

The Australians were in the run-up to a general election and we were all looking forward to getting to Canberra to see the two party leaders in action. Just as the British Labour party were reckoned to have contributed to the Conservative election victory by threatening to increase taxes if elected, the Australian Liberals, equivalent to our Conservative party, were in danger of doing the same thing. They, too, lost the election, against all predictions.

'No, they didn't ask me to comment on the Queen,' I told Alan, 'but the next best thing. They wanted me to talk about Margaret Thatcher.'

'And what did you say about her?' he asked.

'I told them she was on hormone replacement therapy, the same as me. I said it was the secret of her success.' As a junior member of the delegation I had decided to keep off political subjects if at all possible.

'And her downfall?' Alan teased me.

'No. That was down to the boys in her band,' I retorted.

'And one or two of the girls,' said Alan, a reference to Emma Nicholson and Edwina Currie, who had campaigned for Michael Heseltine in the leadership contest.

'I thought they might have asked me about the ERM but they didn't mention it,' I said. Until Black Wednesday, the television people in Australia were more interested in HRT than British politics. We were there for three weeks travelling from state to state meeting umpteen local politicians. This sort of visit is frightfully interesting for the first five days and not quite so diverting for the rest of the time. Some members of our group would get slightly vexed, or perhaps even a little jealous, when they had to attend yet another boring presentation while I swanned off to radio or television studios to strut my stuff.

Although the Australians were, of course, preoccupied with their own election, news of the UK's battle over the ERM and the decline in the Government's ratings back home reached them. We were kept informed by the newspapers that the international money markets were reflecting concern that our economy was in the doldrums and social service spending was in overdrive. There were reports that the markets were beginning to divest themselves of sterling at an increasing pace. The Bank of England, on instructions from the Treasury, was buying it to persuade the markets that the Government was determined not to devalue the pound. But the dam burst on 16 September. The Government no longer had enough foreign currency or gold to buy in all the sterling that was being dumped. They had to give up. The official rate of exchange between sterling and the Deutschmark sank out of its agreed bounds and sterling crashed out of the ERM.

Norman Lamont, the Chancellor, so recently reassuring us in Parliament that the ERM was the best thing that had happened to Britain since D-day, now came on television. 'The Government has decided that sterling is to be allowed to float,' he told the assembled media. Did this remark, I wondered, represent his true sentiments all along? Had the temptation of office previously overcome his innate good judgement and allowed him to continue a policy that was ruining people's lives? The Prime Minister, not to be out-done, joined the chorus of those praising the new arrange-ments, as if it had been his idea all along. Sterling's fall from the ERM wasted billions of the British taxpayers' pounds in buying it at far above its real value.

Now all the media in Australia wanted to hear about from us was the effect of this *débâcle* on the Prime Minister's prospects. It was difficult to avoid giving a straight answer and working my response into an interview on hormone replacement therapy, but I did my best. It went something like this: 'Margaret Thatcher, whose success I attribute to hormone replacement therapy, was opposed to the ERM all along. But she allowed her chancellor, John Major, to coax her into it.'

'Does that mean this treatment rejuvenates your body but not your mind?' asked one smart-ass interviewer.

'Hormone replacement refreshes all the parts which other treatments cannot reach,' I assured him.

I felt I was doing my best for my twin passions of free market and hormone replacement. I just hoped that Alan Howarth wasn't watching at the time.

On Black Wednesday our delegation had arrived in Sydney for the last round of official engagements, after which we were to disperse and make our way back eventually to the UK. Dr Norman Godman, one of the Labour delegates, was looking forward to meeting his wife, who was flying out from the UK to join him at the christening of their first Australian grandchild. I was looking forward to spending ten days visiting Australian friends and relations while a couple of others intended to hop up to the Barrier Reef to survey the underwater scene.

But an urgent message from the Whips in London scuppered all these plans. The Government had called an emergency debate in the House of Commons for 24 September. And there was a three-line whip. Our pleas that our votes – three Labour and three Conservative – would cancel each other out fell on deaf ears. At such times the Whips' office regard it as a sign of their masculinity to turn out a full complement of their troops. So four holidays were ruined.

My office staff telephoned me in Sydney. 'Christopher Gill has called to tell you there will be dinner at Rodin's on the twenty-third to discuss strategy. Will you be back in London by then?'

The idea of meeting my chums was some consolation for my annoyance at being dragged back to London for a debate on a crisis which I thought the Government could have avoided. At least the dinner would provide some lively entertainment and an opportunity to get the inside dope on what had been happening in London in the run-up to the crisis. And I was looking forward to seeing Jim again.

Back in London we were in good spirits. It was wonderful to be proved right. The recession, which was playing havoc with the popularity of the Conservative party, was mainly due, we felt, to the decision to enter the ERM and now the chickens were coming home to roost. Perhaps now the Government would change tack.

Michael was cheerful and had drafted a new early-day motion welcoming the events of Wednesday and urging the Government to promise never again to go back into the Exchange Rate Mechanism. Once again, he called for a fresh start to economic policy.

This time the EDM said that, 'this House welcomes the Government's decision to leave the ERM; and urges a fresh start to economic policy in particular the abandonment of fixed exchange rates and a commitment to sound finance, stable money and the right climate for steady growth.'

It attracted seventy-one signatures. This told us that real opposition to Maastricht, whether tacit or overt, was still strong.

10

STERLING TAKES
A NOSE DIVE

By two o'clock on 24 September, the members' lobby was already milling with disgruntled MPs brought back from their summer retreats. The smell of suntan lotion filled the air. I could hardly recognize some of the pallid characters I had said goodbye to at the beginning of the recess. Now they all seemed ten years younger. All round me small groups grumbled and gossiped: about France and Florence and the international financial crisis. An emergency debate is always exciting but this one had a special attraction for those of us who had been predicting the end of the ERM all along. Euro-fanatics looked distinctly grim. Euro-sceptics positively glowed.

'How are you going to explain this one away?' I asked Hugh Dykes, who was heavily into Europe.

'I don't need to explain. We're the victims of international currency speculators.'

'Not that old chestnut! Can't you do better than that? How about the Americans or the Germans – or even the Bundesbank?' I goaded him.

'Why not the weather?' quipped Tony Marlow, one of our group who was prepared to lay down his political life over the treaty.

'Or sex?' said someone else.

It is rare for the benches in the chamber to be full when the Speaker arrives at 2.30 for prayers but that day they were packed: members were even sitting in the aisles, all the seats having been reserved earlier on. And most unusually, John Major and John Smith were in their places, the first time that I had seen the Prime Minister and the Leader of the Opposition praying together. John Smith's entry was greeted with an enormous cheer and waving of order papers by the Labour MPs to welcome him on his first appearance since becoming their leader. The two front benches exchanged friendly smiles.

The Speaker, Betty Boothroyd, rose to open the debate.

'We now come to the debate on the United Kingdom economic policy—'

'What policy?' shouted Dennis Skinner, notoriously known as the Beast of Bolsover, from his seat on the front bench, below the gangway. 'It's a bloody shambles,' he yelled, to Labour cheers.

'I am delighted to note the House has returned in good mood,' said Betty. This was first-day-back-at-school stuff. 'Before we begin I must announce that I have selected the amendments standing in the name of the Right Honourable and Learned Member, the Leader of the Opposition.'

Here the Labour party burst into fresh cheers.

'Bring back Neil. All is forgiven,' yelled some of the Tories.

'Order, order!' Betty shouted. 'These are important announcements. I expect the co-operation of the House in ensuring I get it,' she said, in her best, stern headmistressy manner.

'The Prime Minister,' she called, and John Major rose to his feet.

This was going to be one of those rare occasions when the front bench on both sides have almost identical policies but have to pretend otherwise. The trick for the Leader of the Opposition is to condemn the other side without admitting that if he was in power he would probably be in the same mess. The Prime Minister's task was to try to get himself out of a hole without admitting that it was he who had dug it. The fun was to see who would be best at defending the indefensible.

'The Leader of the Opposition, whom I warmly welcome to his new responsibilities, was consistent in his support of the Exchange Rate Mechanism,' he began, pointing out that John Smith had egg on his face as well. 'When we joined it, he supported us. When I announced the central rate of exchange, he was generous enough to agree. And when, last week, I said we needed reforms because fault lines had become apparent—'

'You mean an earthquake,' shouted Dennis Skinner, who can always be relied on to liven up a debate.

The Prime Minister allowed himself a smile. 'The Right Honourable and Learned Gentleman agreed with us on the need for reforms. I congratulate him on his consistency. The House has become not just a debating chamber but an echo chamber.'

This was a good start and the Tory benches erupted in laughter and 'hear, hears'.

'Now, of course, we hear most loudly from those people who were critics of the Exchange Rate Mechanism. They come from all sides and every party. My Right Honourable Friend Lord Tebbit, I understand, said the Government was dragged in by the then Chancellor.'

Wow! Was the Prime Minister going to blame Lord Tebbit for the problem? Since Black Wednesday Norman had appeared on rather a lot of television programmes criticizing the Government; I had even seen him on CNN while I was in Australia.

'Now, we all know my Right Honourable Friend Lord Tebbit. He is an old friend of us all. I admire him as a man of great courage, a fighter, a bruiser. He likes to bite your ankles, even if you are not walking up his pathway. Yet even my Right Honourable Friend Lord Tebbit lost many battles with my formidable predecessor. Despite this, according to Lord Tebbit, even my formidable predecessor, whose convictions and firmness of purpose are everywhere admired, was somehow dragged into the Exchange Rate Mechanism by her new chancellor. Ah, yes, I remember it well.' This was a most extraordinary tack for the Prime Minister to take. The House didn't know what to make of it. Was this irony, and did he mean to imply that it was not his decision to go into the ERM – but Margaret Thatcher's?

The Prime Minister's tactics were to blame the collapse of sterling on everything but our own policies: the referendum in Denmark; the referendum in France; the reunification of Germany; speculation against the lira; and, of course, the currency speculators.

'The market, encouraged by injudicious comments about realignment which should never have been made, turned on sterling.' Ah yes, the speculators.

By now, members on both sides of the House were jumping up and down. The Prime Minister, always courteous to people who try to intervene, brushed them away gently. 'I shall give way later,' he told them one after another.

But Tony Benn was particularly persistent, and addicted to the concept of wicked capitalists undermining everything British. 'The Prime Minister has repeatedly told us his object is that we should be at the heart of Europe. Will you please explain how allowing speculators to determine our currency puts this country at the heart of Europe? Isn't it clear that the British, like the Danish and the Irish and the French, should determine what is essentially a political matter in a debate dressed up as an economic debate?' he demanded.

I like Tony Benn. Born with a silver spoon in his mouth, he longs to be mistaken for a horny-handed son of the soil by dressing down in an old grey woolly cardie which he wears under his crumpled suits. The pipe, the lisp and the innate good manners give him away. Nobody but a toff would dream of walking round Parliament dressed like that. I think he's barmy on economics but he is a ferocious defender of women's interests so I am a fan of his. I once appeared with him on *Any Questions* in South Wales during the Alton debate on abortion.

'I absha-lutely agree with everything Teresha shaysh. Women must retain the right to chooshe,' he said. We also shared an interest in having a man and a woman MP for each constituency as a way round the problem of getting more women into parliament.

'We must stop agreeing with each other in public,' I said to him after the programme. 'You'll get me drummed out of the Tories.'

'What do you think it would do to my chances in the Labour party? They think you're a right-wing monster,' he said. We laughed.

Now it was Teddy Taylor's turn to get into the debate.

'To avoid any possible misunderstanding, will the Prime Minister say whether it is the Government's intention to seek to rejoin a fixed exchange rate system?' he asked. Teddy is one of the House's experts on Europe.

The Prime Minister was evasive. 'I have explained to the

House twice that we shall examine whether a system can be made credible. And when we have finished that examination, we will make our decision.'

Euro-sceptics were now jumping up all over the place. Next to catch the Speaker's eye was Nicholas Budgen.

'Will my Right Honourable Friend give way?' The Prime Minister seemed reluctant.

'Give way, give way!' shouted the Labour party, enjoying the spectacle of Tories criticizing Tories.

The excitement and the noise level rose.

'Order, order!' yelled Betty. 'The Prime Minister has made it clear he wants to make a little progress.'

But the Prime Minister had second thoughts. He turned and gave Nick Budgen a smile. 'I will give way to my Honourable Friend,' he said graciously.

Nick Budgen is a slim, birdlike barrister with an analytical mind and, on a good day, a nice line in satire. But that day he was being sober and straightforward.

'Will my Right Honourable Friend the Prime Minister please explain to the House what are the new details that have caught him out so unexpectedly that he requires guidance on them before he can tell the House whether he intends to go back into the Exchange Rate Mechanism?'

'My Honourable Friend has a long-held view that the right thing to do is to let sterling float.'

'Hear, hear!' I shouted, to the frosty stares of Euro-fans seated round me.

'I believe it is time we turned afresh to face directly the whole question of Europe and our place in the European Community. There are three schools of thought. There are people who in their hearts would prefer it if we were not in the Community—'

'Hear, hear!' I called again, warming up to the debate.

'Rubbish!' shouted somebody a few benches in front of me, but without turning round.

'The second school of thought is that European development is inevitable but goes only in one direction. The third school of thought, the one I stand for, is different. It is that it is in the interests of Britain to be part of the development of Europe. I do not mean a walk-on part, I mean a leading role. There are fears throughout Europe that the Community is too centralized, too undemocratic and developing too fast, and that is the policy which Maastricht seeks to put right.'

Cries of 'Rubbish!' greeted this remark from opponents of the treaty. On the Labour benches Peter Shore leaned forward as if he intended to intervene, as did David Winnick and Dale Campbell-Savours. Shouts of 'Give way!' echoed from the supporters of each would-be speaker.

'Order!' shouted Betty. 'Order!' The would-be interveners sat down. But as soon as they were seated Bill Cash, four rows back and at the far end of the chamber, stood up.

'Give way!' the chant broke out again from the Labour benches.

Betty was getting angry. 'Order! Order!' she cried. 'The Prime Minister knows exactly who is standing behind him. If he wants to give way he will do so.'

The Prime Minister did not want to give way to Bill Cash, who had been a thorn in the side of the Government over Europe for many years, but he hesitated and gave way when John Wilkinson, another of our Euro-sceptics, stood up.

'Is my Right Honourable Friend really telling the House that, notwithstanding the fact that two-thirds of the French people did not vote in favour of ratification of the Maastricht treaty, or the fact that the Danes voted against it, and the fact that my Right Honourable Friend will not grant the British people a referendum, the House is somehow to proceed with this extraordinary process?'

John Wilkinson, in his early fifties and typically military, was a man I hardly knew before the Fresh Start group was up and running. As you get older you often fail to recognize people who live next door to you, let alone 650 whom you may occasionally have passed in the members' lobby. An old Etonian from Churchill College, Cambridge, he had held a senior rank in the RAF and is one of the staunchest and most determined members of our group. If I had to go to war, I'd like to have him for my general.

'We are a parliamentary democracy, and the House is the place in which to consider the Bill, line by line and clause by clause,' snapped the Prime Minister. 'Other nations may have a tradition of referendums. That is not our parliamentary tradition and I do not believe it would be acceptable to the House of Commons.'

'Why don't you try it?' shouted Dennis Skinner.

'What about Northern Ireland?'

'The Scots had one!'

'What about '75?' – a reference to the referendum on the European Community held by Harold Wilson.

Now it was Michael Spicer's turn to get in on the act. 'My Right Honourable Friend has expressed the view that the House should make the final decision on the Maastricht Bill. Therefore, will he give consideration to allowing a free vote in the House?'

More 'Hear, hears' from the Euro-sceptics on both sides of the House.

'I believe my Honourable Friend stood at the general election supporting the Conservative manifesto, which indicated that we would bring the Bill before the House,' said the Prime Minister icily. Michael had been Minister for Housing under Margaret Thatcher but resigned from the job when John Major became leader because they were miles apart on Europe and the ERM.

'It is worth reminding ourselves why the Community was built and why we joined it in the first place. Its founders wanted lasting peace in Western Europe and achieved it but they wanted something more —'

'They wanted more of our money,' shouted someone on the opposite benches.

'They wanted our fishing industry,' from the Labour back benches.

'They're a fishy lot.'

'It's a smelly business,' yelled Dennis Skinner, interrupting for the umpteenth time.

Despite his generosity in giving way, the Prime Minister was losing the attention of the House when Jimmy Boyce, Labour member for Rotherham, leapt to his feet.

'On a point of order, Madam Speaker,' he yelled. 'Given that the debate's title is the United Kingdom's economic policy, could you tell us when the Prime Minister is going to get around to discussing that policy?' And he sat down.

Betty stood up. 'As I have not seen the Prime Minister's speech in advance I can only say that the Honourable Member for Rotherham must give the Prime Minister the opportunity to reach that point.'

The Labour party were getting restless: they wanted to hear their new champion tear into the Government. For John Smith, it was important to make a good début. On a good day, and with plenty of time to prepare a speech, he can be an effective performer. This was going to be one of his better days, at least at the start of his speech – until he, too, descended into blaming it all on the speculators.

'This is a government whose economic policy is in tatters, whose credibility is blown, whose incompetence has been exposed. It will no longer do to blame others and it will no longer do to say that their policies will, given time, come right. They have been in power for the longest continuous period in post-war Britain.'

The Tory benches erupted with cries of 'Hear, hear!', 'Get on your bike, John', 'You'll have to do better than that.'

The House was now in uproar but, with the help of the microphone, John Smith bellowed above it. 'In the course of a few weeks the one policy with which the Prime Minister was uniquely and personally associated and which he appears to have been most proud of, has been blown apart, and with it has gone for ever a claim by the Prime Minister or the party he leads to economic competence. He is the devalued prime minister of a devalued government.'

The Labour party went wild cheering and waving their order papers: their new leader had come up trumps. The Leader of the Opposition resumed his seat, a broad smile on his broad face, his balding head glowing as a result of his exertions under the television lights, his small brown eyes darting from side to side, looking almost surprised at his success. Margaret Beckett, dressed neatly in red, leaned over to pat his arm. His Chief Whip leaned across her to congratulate him. He had carried out his first assignment well.

I spotted Michael Spicer and hurried after him, catching up with him in the members' lobby.

'That was a good intervention,' I said. 'But you didn't

get a straight answer from the PM. Having something in the manifesto doesn't mean you can't have a free vote on it. I don't know about you but I made sure my election address made it clear that I was for an independent Britain, not closer ties with Europe.'

Michael nodded. 'What are you doing now? Shall we go to the tea room? I'm getting up another EDM urging the Government to drop economic union with Europe. Will you sign?'

We made our way out of the members' lobby and along the corridor to the tea room. It was already full but we found two places and he put the EDM, which he'd already drafted, in front of me.

'Anyone else like to sign my EDM?'

I went to pick up the paper which I'd just signed but it had glued itself to the table. 'Ugh! If you rest your arms on these tables you have to peel them off carefully or you leave your skin behind,' I said with distaste.

'I've never noticed,' said one of the men.

'You wouldn't. You chaps are always protected by your grey suits. These tables need a good scrub. I'm going to put it in the complaints book.'

I brought the complaints book back to the table. The last entry was by Simon Burns. It said baldly, 'Mice seen in tea room. Get rid of them at once.'

'I've never seen mice in here,' I said.

'Haven't you ever had one of their meat sandwiches?' asked Geoffrey Dickens. 'You can tell if they're fresh, the tails are still moving.'

'They serve them *à la carte* or *table d'hôte* in the members' dining room,' said Donald Thompson, ex-Minister of Agriculture.

'And in pies in the strangers' dining room,' said someone else.

The whole table was laughing.

'Do you know the joke about the man who went into a pub and was offered a pie, a pint and a woman for seventy-five pence?' said Geoffrey. '"What's in the pie?" he asked.'

Geoffrey is one of the House of Commons' great characters and much in demand as an after-dinner speaker. We all jot down his old jokes and recycle them to lighten our own speeches.

I was keeping an eye on the monitor screen in the corner. Edward Heath's name came up. Immediately, the tea room began to empty as we moved back to the chamber. It was interesting to see the old boy in action again after so many years in cold storage.

Sir Edward rose from his seat on the front bench, like a great bear from a pit. Virtually unemployable since 1975, he was suddenly back in the limelight and preening himself now that he had some work to do, although it was no substitute for a government of his own to run.

'In his speech the Prime Minister reaffirmed that he believes the Maastricht agreement is good for Europe and for Britain. I strongly agree with him,' he said, his double chin wobbling, his deep voice reverberating. 'He has reaffirmed that it does not exclude a return to the ERM at some future date. He's also reaffirmed that in no circumstances will he agree to a referendum. In that he is absolutely right. I was glad the Leader of the Opposition succeeded in carrying at least his national executive committee with him in agreeing that there would be no referendum. There is no reason why this should be.'

'We're still working on that,' shouted Dennis Skinner, who had opposed European union all his political life.

'I don't think that the Honourable Member will have much success,' Heath pontificated.

'The Right Honourable Gentleman should not put any bets on it,' retorted Skinner. Dennis prides himself on being a House of Commons man. He is always there at half past two to claim his seat but he doesn't join in prayers: he doesn't believe in it. I've never seen him in a suit, always the same black and white tweed jacket and grey trousers.

There was a time, in the distant past, when support from Heath would be the kiss of death for a prime minister but, we were beginning to learn, John Major had a great deal more in common with Heath's views than we had realized. Now, when making a speech, the Prime Minister often paid him compliments. For Heath it was proof that there was life after death and he was basking in the novelty.

The debate wore on until 9.30 p.m. The Chancellor of the Exchequer, Norman Lamont, rose to defend his actions over the last few weeks. In the past eight days he had done a complete somersault: from claiming that the ERM was immutable he now declared that it was expendable. This was difficult enough for someone who really believed in the ERM, but I don't think Norman did: I feel sure in his heart he is a sceptic, just like us. Neither he nor Michael Portillo, his second-in-command, would have supported the ERM or Maastricht, if they hadn't had to toe the party line.

But Norman is an old-stager with nifty footwork developed over a number of years as a minister and he gave a nimble performance. I thought he was always much better in a debate in the chamber than his television performances suggested. He ducked and dived. He gave a logical but not credible explanation for his U-turn. He, too, blamed it all on the markets and those poor old speculators.

'Sound money, free enterprise, light regulation and less government are the principles on which we fought the election. Nothing that has happened in recent days changes our commitment to those objectives or the fact that we are the only party that bases its policies on them.'

His peroration over, he resumed his seat, the obligatory 'Hear, hears' ringing in his ears.

We filed into the voting lobbies. The Labour motion condemning the Government was defeated. The Government won its motion with a majority of twenty-six.

Next day, however, Michael Spicer's EDM, which condemned the government's policy, attracted 71 Tory signatures which means that 45 people voted with the Government but against their conscience.

11

CASH'S ARMY

B y now our group was well established and morale was high as we entered the next stage of our battle. We had learned a lot about each other as well as the Government's tactics and we were ready for the committee stage when the Bill would be fought over line by line in a committee consisting of the whole House. This is a relatively unusual procedure. Most Bills are examined in small, cross-party groups of MPs in one of the committee rooms upstairs. For a Bill to be taken through committee on the floor of the chamber is an acknowledgement of the seriousness of the changes in our constitution that this Bill proposed. Every MP would be given the opportunity to contribute to the debate.

The paving debate called for an orator; the committee stage required a lawyer's mind. There were several lawyers in our group but no one knew the intricacies of the treaty as intimately as Bill Cash. He knew by heart every line of every clause and every sub-clause. He seemed to enjoy unravelling it to reveal its most intimate meaning. For me trying to grasp its implications was like swimming through porridge and I felt a certain sympathy for Kenneth Clarke, who once admitted he had not read it.

Once Bill gave me a long and detailed explanation of the treaty.

'I am no wiser now than when you started,' I told him, in exasperation.

'Possibly not,' he answered, recalling a famous remark made by the lawyer F. E. Smith, who became Lord Birkenhead, 'but you are far better informed.' A tall, lanky lawyer with spectacles and thick grey hair, through which he frequently ran his fingers, he is one of the intellectual power-houses of the group.

To be effective on these occasions you must know your facts or have them supplied to you in briefing notes, unless you are Bill Cash or Richard Shepherd, a natural orator with an inborn hatred for and an encyclopaedic knowledge of European legislation all the way back to 1972. On the other hand, it is equally effective to be like Teddy Taylor, an aggressive street fighter with an innate feeling for the mean ing of nationhood who can speak passionately off the top of his head. Then there was Tony Marlow, a kamikaze pilot given to interrupting everyone else's speeches if he hears something he can tear to shreds. Or else you are like me and need regular briefing notes on each stage of the debate in order to follow it. These came from two sources: Teddy Taylor's research assistant and the indefatigable Bill Cash's private army.

With a small group of voluntary helpers, which included one of the best informed anti-Maastricht lawyers in the country, Martin Howe, Bill had taken up temporary occupation at No. 17 Great College Street, an elegant eighteenth-century house owned by Lord McAlpine. It was also used by Margaret Thatcher immediately after she was so unceremoniously ousted from Downing Street. The poet Percy Bysshe Shelley once lived there but now it harboured a hard-nosed and dedicated bunch of activists who were determined to fight for what they thought was right. One commentator described the set-up in admiring tones: 'Within this elegant house resides what must surely be the most audacious, elaborate and best-financed parliamentary campaign ever mounted by dissident Tory MPs still in receipt of their party's whip.'

From this base the highly professional team turned out computer-printed briefing material gleaned from their own research and a national network of sympathetic QCs, economists and business advisers. It was all collated and distributed to Euro-sceptics, the better to improve their contribution to the debate. We got it every few days, both the policy implications of clauses in the Maastricht Bill and the tactical implications of defying government Whips on particular votes. It was all fascinating fodder for me, and especially useful when I had to deal with the implications of the more arcane aspects of the treaty.

Bill's wife, Biddy, who looks like a model and wears Chanel suits with pelmet-length skirts – you would never believe she is the mother of grown-up children – appeared to take charge of the team. Highly political and a tireless worker, she also organized some excellent supper parties, with dishes like Maastricht pie supplied by the local butcher from someone's constituency. Everyone who was anyone in the anti-Maastricht wing of the media turned up: Charles Moore of the *Daily Telegraph*, Andrew Alexander of the *Daily Mail*, Paul Johnson, Russell Lewis, Leo Price, Martin Howe and, on one occasion, Margaret Thatcher. Her presence still creates a buzz of excitement around a room. Sometimes people came from the City; diplomats or members of trade associations also came to our get-togethers, people who supported us in private but did not like to admit publicly that they were as sceptical about the treaty as we all were. I have no idea why they felt it necessary to keep their views a secret.

Occasionally the cameras were allowed in: Bill reckoned it would be good for our image if people in the country could see we were just a jolly bunch of normal people and not the wreckers we were sometimes portrayed as. The camaraderie was good, so was the food. They were some of the best social occasions I can remember since entering Parliament. It all helped to cement us into one of the most effective fighting forces anyone could ever remember in the history of Parliament.

12

BRIGHTON ROCKS

E veryone who is anyone goes to the party conferences. It is a chance for editors, political pundits and ministers to meet informally over drinks or dinner, for the party faithful to mingle with MPs and the media, for an aspiring politician to make a spell-binding speech, for pressure groups to holler and wave their fists as delegates come and go. It's a wonderful seaside jamboree.

The lavish parties of yesteryear have more or less vanished. Lord McAlpine used to hold the best ones when we would be served with lobster and champagne. Now they are hosted by Jeffrey Archer, who served cottage pie last year . . .

Lord King presided at the British Airways bash as if he were, indeed, a king. He used to give us a china mug just like the Coronation mugs you were given as a child as a leaving present. Lord King used to start telling jokes and forget the punchline half-way through. The story would tail off and he'd start mumbling and bumbling and his sidekick had to prompt him with the end of the joke. The most intellectual party was the *Spectator*'s, when Charles Moore was editor, and Associated Newspapers always had a lively affair. I had dinner at one of them with Sir David English when he was all sweetness and light, yet a month later one of his newspapers wrote a vituperative article about me and Bill Cash.

They may pretend they can't stand MPs but when they

want material for their columns journalists buzz round you like bees round a honeypot.

There are some splendid characters among the media, some of whom are so in love with themselves they are risible. One such is Peregrine Worsthorne. We used to pull his leg unmercifully but he was so blinded by his own brilliance he didn't see it. Once, talking about the man on the Clapham omnibus having no manners, he said there should be conscription again because the army civilized people.

'Don't you think,' I suggested, 'we should have conscription for compulsory domestic service then the lower orders could work for their betters and learn manners from them?'

'Do you know, Teresa, I think that is an awfully good idea,' he said. He doesn't just have one, he speaks with a pound of plums in his mouth. It was uproarious. He was deadly serious.

There are always scandals – naughty boys using the conference as an excuse to have amorous assignations with naughty girls, party apparatchiks trying to score points off each other, quarrels behind closed doors. There was a humdinger of a slanging match between Norman Tebbit and Kenneth Clarke which became known as the Clash of the Titans. At one of the posh parties Norman Tebbit was pontificating about some aspect of the treaty and trying to nail Clarke about his and the government's stand on something. Their voices were getting louder and louder so you couldn't help but overhear it all. Eventually Clarke, in exasperation, admitted he hadn't read the bloody thing. But, then, he seems to have a problem absorbing the written word. I was told that at one dinner being held by a newspaper editor and his political team, Ken, accompanied by his wife, Gillian, arrived apologizing profusely. 'I have to go to do a *Newsnight* broadcast at ten o'clock, I'm terribly sorry,' he told his hosts. 'I really am frightfully sorry.'

At about nine thirty the young woman from the hotel who was serving the meal in their private suite took a phone call and handed Mr Clarke a note. He glanced at it, put it in his pocket and said, 'Gosh, I'm really terribly sorry but I've got to go now. Are you going to stay?' he asked Gillian.

She nodded and he rushed out of the room and down the corridor. A few minutes later he reappeared. Apparently he read the note in the lift and it was to say the broadcast had been cancelled. 'Gosh, I'm most frightfully sorry,' he said again. They all thought he was nuts.

Lining you up for a broadcast and then cancelling it again because they have found someone else bigger and better is an exasperating habit of television people. I was asked to do a slot on the last day of the conference, Friday morning, with Sir Robin Day and I cancelled half a dozen things in order to do it. When they told me it had all been changed and I wasn't needed after all, I hit the roof and I told Sir Robin what I thought of him in no uncertain terms.

His bow-tie was trembling and he said, 'Leave me alone, leave me alone. I won't be fit to do the broadcast.'

'I won't leave you alone until you apologize,' I replied. I was livid, not because the broadcast was not going ahead but because I had rearranged so many appointments.

His producer, who was clearly stunned at what he perceived as my impertinence, tried to push me away. 'Don't upset Sir Robin before he goes on air,' he squeaked.

But I was equally determined to get it off my chest. 'You're a chauvinist. You've dumped me to get a man on instead,' I accused him.

'I'm not a chauvinist, far from it,' Sir Robin protested.

But I bet it was true because a – male – minister, David Young, who was always putting his puddings out for treacle, did the broadcast in the end and as far as they were concerned, yours truly could take a running jump. Charming. It makes me mad. You can hear them all the time at the conference: 'You must come on to my programme, old boy.' 'Certainly, old boy, I'd love to.'

Anyway, all's well that ends well. Next day Sir Robin dropped a card through my letter-box with a very gentlemanly apology.

'What's the conference going to be about this year?' a television reporter asked me as we sat side by side in the first-class compartment.

'Europe,' I said. 'And the economy.'

'The economy, certainly, but I'm not sure about Europe. Don't most Tories find it a turn-off?' he asked.

'Most of them try to ignore it but I think they've got the message that it means monetary union and that means higher interest rates. They're certainly aware that we've dropped out of the ERM.'

Outside the window, the green countryside of Sussex streamed by, a stark contrast to the Australian landscape I had left barely two weeks ago. So much had happened in politics since then.

Almost daily the serious press was reporting polls showing the decline in support for the Tory party and for the Prime Minister. Undoubtedly the recession had a lot to do with it but in my constituency they summed up their feelings by saying he should sort out our domestic problems first. This may have been unfair but when people are worried about their jobs, their savings and their mortgages, they quite reasonably blame the Government.

The Prime Minister was having a rough time because he was obsessed with his European policies. He would not read the signs. I wish he would come round and read my postbag. Black Wednesday, or White Wednesday as we prefer to call it because it is the best thing that could have happened to the British economy, could also have saved him. He even had a scapegoat in the Chancellor, Norman Lamont, who could be made to carry the can for it. Rough justice, but that's politics.

'Why do you think the Prime Minister clings so rigidly to monetary union?' the reporter asked me.

'The Treasury, I suppose, and the Foreign Office. He's done most of his Cabinet service in those offices and they're both in love with foreigners.'

I flicked through the conference prospectus. On Tuesday afternoon there was to be a full-scale debate on Europe. That would be interesting. I glanced through the supplement on fringe meetings. I was speaking at one or two of them including Charter 88, an organization that wanted a written constitution. One or two pro-referendum groups were having meetings and a group of Young Conservatives, supporters of Fresh Start, was launching a petition calling for a referendum. Michael Spicer had a hand in that.

I was looking forward to staying at the Norfolk Resort Hotel on the front, close to the conference centre. It was owned by my new friend Lily Feld. She and I became pen-pals when she wrote a splendid article on the right to smoke herself to death if she wanted to. I wrote to congratulate her. She came to the House of Commons to have lunch with me in a white Rolls-Royce she had saved up for all her life. I love people who claim the right to go to hell in their own way. That's real democracy.

As the taxi made the turn into the side street which led down to the front, we were stopped by a policeman. 'You can't go this way. There's a bomb alert.' Brighton had had a terrible experience at the 1984 conference when the Grand Hotel was bombed. John Wakeham lost his wife and Margaret Tebbit was paralysed. Norman still suffers from the injuries he sustained. I don't know how he can bear to come back again but rumours were flying around that he would speak in the Europe debate.

I paid the taxi driver and walked round to the back of the hotel to find a way in. I made my way into the garage and found a door. It was locked. I hammered on it. After a short while a voice called out, 'Who is it?'

'I'm a guest. I've got a booking. The police have got the street cordoned off and I can't get in at the front of the hotel.'

'I am not supposed to let anyone in. There's a bomb alert.'

'I know that. But I can't stand here for an hour waiting till it's over. Is Mrs Feld in the hotel? Tell her it's Teresa Gorman. I'm a friend of hers.'

I waited a little longer. Then the door was opened and pushed out towards me.

'I'm not supposed to do this. But Madam says you're to come in.' And he locked the door after me.

Lily was waiting to greet me in the hall.

Now in her seventies, but wonderfully well preserved, she looks like a fashion model, elegantly dressed. She had paid careful attention to her make-up. And, of course, she was smoking.

'Welcome. It's lovely to have you. I've got some other friends staying for the conference. I hope we're going to have a good week.'

Getting a room in a decent hotel close to the conference centre requires the kind of forward planning that is not in my nature. Some people book their hotels years ahead. The last time we were at Brighton I recalled sharing a rented flat of indescribable squalor with my friend Patricia Rawlings. But it was right on the front and we were only two blocks away from the Grand.

'I hope to God we're not going to have any trouble with the IRA this year.'

'Not if the police have anything to do with it. They've investigated every room, every nook and cranny and every drain-hole in the whole of Brighton. There isn't room to hide a cigarette end.' She laughed.

Security is now so tight at conferences that it can take an hour to get in so it is important either to go early to miss the crush or wait till mid-morning and hope it has died down. Conferences, these days, attract as many as five thousand delegates, plus the media from all over the world. Even so, that is a tiny number compared with how many people watch at home. It's hardly surprising they are so carefully staged to get the message across to that wider audience.

On the day of the European debate, I had agreed to talk to a coffee morning of the Hove Conservatives. My research assistant, Brian Oxley, lives in the area and he fixed up the visit. At ten thirty he picked me up and drove me through the morning sunshine along the front to a neat suburban house in Hove. It was full to overflowing. I moved around the room, shaking hands and having a word with everyone.

'We are very glad you came.'

'It's good of you to spare the time.'

'We are looking forward to your talk,' said the hostess.

'I'm delighted to be here. Brian has told me what a grand job you're doing. You've got a lot of people here today, which is encouraging. You would think to read the papers that the Conservative party couldn't fill a broom cupboard these days.'

It was my job to cheer up the faithful and rally them round the party. Whatever I thought, and said, about Maastricht, it was up to me to make them feel that working for the Conservative party was worthy of the time they put in. People make fun of these occasions, I expect because they are mainly for women. In fact these people are the backbone of the party.

'What would you like me to talk about? I can talk about most things – the economy, or being a woman in Parliament, anything you fancy.'

'I think everyone here is worried about the state of the party. Everything seems to be going wrong for us.'

One of the nicest things about being an MP is playing to an audience like this. You don't need a grand speech, or any speech at all; you just need to be warm and friendly and try to throw in a few funny stories.

An hour and a half later we were steaming back to the conference hall.

'Thanks for doing that. They loved it. They don't often get an MP for a coffee morning.'

'And some of them brought their husbands,' I said,

because that was unusual. One happened to be a doctor who had written to me about my ten-minute-rule Bill on tattooing. He is one of the country's leading authorities and I remember quoting from an article of his when I did the Bill. Small world.

Without a ministry to run, or even a backbench committee (I hate committees), I had made a bit of a speciality of ten-minute-rule Bills. Twice a week at about half past three, in prime television time, a backbencher can claim ten minutes in which to present a Bill to the House on almost any subject. I had been doing them regularly ever since 1987 when I was elected.

I'd introduced one for the privatization of the post office, compulsory pooper scoopers, tax relief for the cost of childcare, and another to give rights to women co-habitees who at present have no rights over their children or their communal property if the man they are living with kicks them out. Six months ago, when I discovered that several cases on the long-term waiting lists were for tattoo removal, I moved a Bill calling for people who got themselves tattooed to take out insurance to cover the cost of its removal. After all, the health service is for people who are ill, not for people who want to mutilate themselves. All of these Bills are merely window dressing in parliamentary terms. But sometimes they attract the attention of the parliamentary press and creep into legislation.

By now we had reached the conference centre. Inside the foyer I was approached by a young woman reporter from independent television.

'Are you going to be in the conference for Norman Tebbit's speech?' she asked me.

'You bet. I imagine everyone else will be too.'

'Where will you be sitting? We might want to cover your reactions.'

'Heaven knows, I imagine it'll be a packed house and there'll be plenty of drama for you to film. Most of it from the platform.' I laughed.

Speaking at the party conference from the floor is meant to be reserved for the rank and file supporters. It can also give an airing to a would-be candidate. But sitting members and party grandees are not encouraged. I recall a conference while Margaret Thatcher was Prime Minister, when Edward Heath was called to speak from the floor. His remarks went down like a lead balloon. But someone with his status, or the status of Lord Tebbit who was going to hi-jack the conference this afternoon, could hardly be denied the opportunity to speak.

I expect the conference organizers could have wished for a TV blackout for the opening ceremony. Brighton's Labour Mayor, Mrs Gill Sweeting, wearing her conference hat in deference to her audience, forgot her manners and delivered a broadside about the lack of government money flowing to the resort. No one could recall a similar occasion when the hostess insulted the guests before they could get their teeth into the first course. Fortunately for the Tories, Dame Elaine Kellett-Bowman, MP, was sitting in the audience close enough to give her what-for. 'This is a party political broadcast,' she said rather loudly. Platform heads spun her way. When Mrs Sweeting asked for more cash, 'I hope you don't get it,' said the Dame. And when the conference chairman politely thanked the Mayor and gave her a bunch of flowers, 'What for?' Kellett-Bowman demanded. There's nothing like a Dame when it comes to defending Tory honour. But this little opener set the tone for the rest of the conference. We were in for four days of fireworks.

The debate was opened, as always, by a delegate presenting the motion which had been selected for debate. As usual, it was suitably anodyne, uncontroversial, and in support of government policy. It attracted an unusually high level of audience reaction, some cheering, others booing. I distinctly heard some hissing when Tristan Garel-Jones joined the government ministers sitting on the platform.

'After the opening speakers I shall call the following names to the rostrum. Will these people please come to the front of the hall so they can get to the rostrum quickly when they are called,' said the chairman.

He read out two or three names and then Lord Tebbit's. A cheer went up. Delegates stood to applaud when his turn came, something I had never seen in seventeen years of attending party conferences.

In a speech in which he declared the Government was in desperate trouble he offered only qualified support for the Prime Minister's policies. Since once being a supporter of John Major's – he campaigned for him in his bid for the leadership – there had been a falling out between them. In the Commons' debate on Black Wednesday, the Prime Minister said something about Norman being 'the kind of man who bit your ankles even when you are not walking up his pathway.' Perhaps he meant it as a joke but it backfired spectacularly. Norman is not known as a semi-house-trained polecat for nothing.

Elevation to the Lords liberates the tongue, and Norman went from being polite about the Prime Minister to speculating publicly on his future – not because he disliked him as a man, but because he felt his policies were out of touch with the rank and file of the Conservative party. This prognostication did not give him any pleasure. Indeed, he made it quite clear that he was immensely sad about it. 'I will support you whenever you pursue policies to restore our economy, preserve our rights in these isles to manage our affairs for ourselves in our interests,' he said. Now he told loyal Tories, 'In 1987 I believed my work in politics was done and for reasons which you will understand I could decently retire to care for my family. I never intended to speak at conference again. But speak today I must. The Government is in desperate trouble.'

On the platform John Major and Douglas Hurd looked as if they had a slice of lemon in their mouths. Norman's every remark was greeted with wild cheering. Although a meaningless vote in favour of the government's policies would be engineered at the end of the debate, Norman's speech would be the subject of every news bulletin for the rest of the day. 'I hope, Prime Minister, you will stand by your chancellor. After all, it was not Norman Lamont's decision to enter the ERM. He did his best to make the unworkable work. The cost in lost jobs, bankruptcies, repossessed homes, the terrible wounds inflicted on industry, have been savage. But we established our credentials as good Europeans,' he added sarcastically. 'Now that we are out of the Deutschmark straitjacket we are free to pursue policies in our own national interest. And not before time.

'Since Maastricht, a great tide of opinion has begun to flow against the federalists, not just here but in Denmark and in France and in Germany, too. This conference wants policies for Britain first, Britain second and Britain third. Politics, like charity, begins at home.'

The audience was roused to fever pitch, they loved him.

'Do we want to be citizens of European union, do we want a single currency, do we want other countries interfering in our immigration controls?' he asked the audience. To each question they shouted, 'No!' The conference went wild.

Matthew Parris reported in next day's *Times* that he sat next to a Tory MP with a minor job in the Government who began growling

> a sort of 'Hear, hear' noise but without opening his mouth so that no one could see him. When the speech was over he joined the clapping enthusiastically but kept his hands under the seat in front so this would not be visible to the cameras or to the platform.
>
> 'Is the Prime Minister looking my way?'
>
> 'No,' I said. At this point he raised his hands above the parapet and clapped even louder.

After Norman, the speakers who had come to the conference to support Europe didn't have a chance. Shouts of 'Never!' 'Rubbish!' 'Bollocks!' greeted them.

It is something I never thought I'd see at a Tory party conference and something we did not see at Blackpool, during the Labour conference which was held the week before. Ours was a real debate.

13

WHIPPING UP

The long and tortuous path to the paving debate, so-called because it paves the way to the main debate, which many commentators thought was totally unnecessary, began with Neil Kinnock. By then a backbencher again, he demanded a written report on the significance of Denmark's unexpected rejection of the Maastricht treaty. The Prime Minister should have told him to get on his bike. But, amazingly, he offered a debate.

This meant a delay before moving the Bill on to the committee stage, a most unusual thing to do, and the Whips advised against it. If the vote were lost the Government would have to drop the Bill.

The Prime Minister was probably relying on the fact that the Liberal Democrats wanted the Bill as much as he did and would vote with the Government. But the Labour party would seize the opportunity, and in the event did, to embarrass the Government by voting against it. To the Euro-rebels this was a heaven-sent opportunity. By voting in the same lobby as Labour we could ditch the Bill once and for all. From that day on the fourteen Whips had their work cut out. Their task was to get John Major off the hook and they used every trick in the book.

Journalists call the Whips 'the usual channels'. Enoch Powell called them the sewers of Parliament, necessary but not very nice.

The world has heard of Numbers 10 and 11 Downing Street, but the real powerhouse is Number 12 where the Chief Whip, currently Richard Ryder, lives. Here his exclusively male coterie meets to make or break careers. Normally they get together once a week but during this Maastricht crisis I wouldn't mind betting they did so daily, if not hourly, so desperate were they to counteract our growing influence.

Membership of the Whips' office is a fast track to becoming a minister. Very few of them stay long, except the Machiavellian Tristan Garel-Jones whose nickname when he was there was the Prince of Darkness. He used to sit in the middle of a web of intrigue and, it was said, no one got their promotion without their MoT certificate, Mate of Tristan. When he became premier, John Major made him a junior foreign minister in charge of Maastricht – and we changed his parliamentary nickname to the Member for Madrid Central. He had spent part of his childhood there and has a Spanish wife.

The Whips' offices in the House of Commons lead out of the members' lobby opposite the entrance to the chamber, the Government on one side, Opposition on the other. Whoever wins the election gets the best set of offices. A carved oak door leads into a corridor with, first, a large common room containing a dozen desks where ordinary backbenchers are free to enter – so long as they don't mind half a dozen suspicious pairs of eyes looking up at them. 'What are you up to now?' they seem to say.

Each desk is submerged in letters and documents. A small, elderly sofa stands along one wall, usually covered in newspapers. At the far end is the door which leads to the Chief Whip's office where backbenchers only enter by appointment, or when summoned.

The first time I was called in by the then Chief Whip, Tim Renton, I really thought the news of my promotion had come at last! Alas, his pained expression told me I was in for a wigging. Apparently I'd written something rude in the *Sunday Times* which he thought unhelpful. 'The newspapers are only interested if I say something cheeky,' I told him plaintively.

'But we would prefer you to say something constructive,' he said firmly. 'Don't you realize your remarks can be bad for the party's image?'

My postbag said otherwise, but I bit my tongue. They had never allowed a woman to be a Whip in the Tory party and that is bad for the party's image too. The Labour party have had them for ages. Everyone in our Whips' office has to agree about a new appointment so if just one man there doesn't like the idea of a woman storming their male bastion, he only has to say no and she's had it. It's called being blackballed.

One of the Whips, Bob Hughes, a smart young man in a hurry and a dripping wet, was always being ticked off by the Speaker for shouting abuse from a sitting position. He organized the ten-minute-rule Bills before me and he helped to manage the putsch against Bill Cash to get him off the backbench Committee on European Affairs. He came into Parliament at the same time as me and promptly volunteered his services to Edward Heath as his factotum and bag-carrier; as if Heath was still Prime Minister. Soon after the 1992 election he was made a Whip, a sure sign that the pro-Europeans were in the ascendant.

The Whips have a way of hovering about or sitting near enough to overhear conversations. On one classic occasion after a particularly acrimonious debate when we went into the main bar, David Lightbown came in and stalked around the room. Then he plonked himself at a table within listening distance his ears flapping like those of an elephant in distress. We switched immediately to discussing our holiday plans.

Although many of the Whips behaved at all times with courtesy and politeness, some seemed to lose all sense of civilized behaviour. James Cran was once called in by deputy Chief Whip David Heathcoat-Amory and subjected to what he considered an extraordinary attack of profanity. James walked out saying he was not prepared to be talked to like a child or sworn at. It was more distressing coming from Heathcoat-Amory rather than one of the Whips you expected thuggish behaviour from because he was thought to be a right-wing sympathizer.

I don't want to give the impression that they're all ruthless. My own Whip, Sydney Chapman, is a darling. He represents Chipping Barnet, between Margaret Thatcher's and Cecil Parkinson's old seats. When Sydney had the job of ticking me off he'd say to me, 'I am not trying to change your views about the treaty. I just want you to understand the seriousness of what you're doing.' He was trying to be firm and cross with me and he's such a nice man, I felt bad too.

'I haven't made up my mind but there's no way I'm going to vote to land the country with this treaty,' I said firmly.

He looked so uncomfortable when he had to tick me off, but I just wanted to cuddle him.

He shook his head chidingly as if exasperated with my behaviour. 'I hope you will think very carefully about what you are doing, that's all,' he ended feebly. I hated to upset him. When he was the Whip in charge of accommodation, he got me a really splendid new office, the first one I've had since I've been in the House.

The Whips are as secretive as the Masons. What goes on behind that oak door is never revealed, unless they want it to be, of course. They go in for news management on a scale that would do credit to MI5, the CIA and the KGB combined. When I read a vitriolic article about the Euro-rebels in the *Mail on Sunday*, I felt in my bones that the Prince of Darkness had a hand in it.

The *Mail* group, previously anti-Maastricht, began to throw its weight behind the Government. On the Sunday before the paving debate, under the pseudonym of Charles Cowley, the *Mail on Sunday* published an article which went right over the top.

Charles Cowley called us a 'repugnant alliance of Major haters . . . who had crawled out from under their stones to launch a relentless political and personal campaign against their leader'. He went on, 'They live in the largely mythical past with dreams of restoring their queen, nay goddess, to glory.'

The rest of the article went on in the same vein accusing us of everything from blind prejudice and a loathing of foreigners to driving out Japanese businessmen! I came in for some special venom. 'So addicted is Mrs Gorman to camera-induced ecstasy we must regard her as a suitable case for detoxification . . . Nightly she appears trilling the same string of political platitudes on television. She must be camped out under plastic sheeting on the doorstep of the BBC in White City, so instantly available is she with a rent-a-quote . . .'

His criticism of Bill Cash was just as extreme. 'William Cash, MP, who seems to appear on TV screens more frequently than the BBC logo itself . . . although the logo is far more animated and charismatic . . . constantly inflicts his relentless anti-Maastricht views on us with such monotonal repetitiveness that one wonders if he is a reconstructed Dalek rather than a member of the human species.'

The whole thing was so outrageous you couldn't take it seriously. As Sir David English, chairman of the group that owns the *Mail on Sunday*, lives around the corner from me in Cowley Street, and his middle name is Charles, I did wonder if he had written the article, hence the pseudonym. But I don't bear him a grudge. I wrote him a nice little postcard thanking him for his kind words and popped it through his letter-box. It was splendid stuff. But I noticed the article dwelt on my so-called personal vanity instead of my sincerely held opinions.

If the Whips were working overtime on their pals in the press, they were not malingering over the job of whipping their charges into line either. They took to that with a vengeance, going for the jugular whenever they felt the need arise. Like Rottweilers, they looked for the most vulnerable area of the anatomy and sank in their teeth.

14

LAST SUPPER

Tension was running high. The dirty tricks campaign had been going on for days now. People were subjected to the nice-nasty technique employed by Whips to secure a Yes vote for Maastricht in what was seen by the Government as its tightest corner yet. Every tactic in the political persuader's lexicon from the extremely crude to the cunningly subtle had been used.

The Prime Minister is fond of recalling his tough training in Lambeth as a political combatant. That week, since he returned from a trip to Cairo where he attended the anniversary ceremony of the battle of El Alamein, he had encouraged his lieutenants to wage war on his enemies. The anti-EC hardheads, he called us. And he soft-soaped those Euro-rebels who weren't 100 per cent sure what to do. They knew the treaty was bad for the country but they could be induced to put their own interests first.

The following day's paving debate was widely construed as a vote of confidence in his leadership: if the Government lost, could John Major remain as leader? Sir George Gardiner, who regards the Maastricht Bill as a suicide pact which Tories should reject, put it succinctly: 'The Prime Minister's survival is now at stake.'

Our meeting, variously billed as the Last Supper or the Night before Alamo, was scheduled for six o'clock in room 21 on the committee floor.

Each time the door opened and a new face appeared a small cheer went up. As more and more people arrived we began to relax. I looked round the room.

'Welcome,' said Michael Spicer. 'Come in. Join the club.' Then, to Walter Sweeney, 'We thought David Lightbown might have had you for tea. He was reported to have shared a teacake with you earlier in the afternoon.'

Walter smiled. Victor of the Vale of Glamorgan, who had overturned a Labour majority of over 6000 in the 1992 election, he had the smallest majority in the country, 19, and was bawled out by the heavyweight Tory Whip in the middle of the members' tea room. I was pleased to see they hadn't frightened him into ditching us. He is obviously not someone easily intimidated by bullying, I thought.

Michael Clark, Robert Jones and Warren Hawksley joined us.

Our Whips, Christopher Gill and James Cran, exchanged glances and compared notes. Someone in the room must have been sent by the Whips, but who? Who was the Judas?

Ivan Lawrence came in. He's fiftyish and stockily built. As usual his blond hair was just a bit too long for a QC. It gave him a slightly raffish air. He was still dressed for court in striped trousers, black jacket and one of those striped shirts with a white collar attached. He was one of the most powerful debaters in the House, addressing it as if he were in court. Strong on law and order, we all thought he would have been made Attorney General after the last election. Instead, he was given a knighthood, often a consolation prize.

John Biffen arrived, quietly spoken, unassuming but a heavyweight none the less. Ex-cabinet minister and former Leader of the House, he had upset Margaret and she sacked him. A pity: when he spoke the House listened. His balanced views and his long experience in politics were invaluable to us.

Next came Sir Peter Tapsell, historian and banker. A giant of a man in every way, with a background on the left of the party, he should have made it to the Cabinet long ago. Tall, imperious, with a halo of greying curls around his high, domed head, I often thought if I had to run up Mount Olympus to deliver a message to Zeus, I'd expect him to look like Peter Tapsell.

His political experience went back to before he became an MP in the 1950s when he worked for Sir Anthony Eden. His contacts with MPs who lived through Chamberlain's years of appeasement and throughout Churchill's war leadership strongly colour his views, as does his upbringing in the 1930s.

The speeches he made were the best I have ever heard and will strike a chord with ordinary people in Britain, no matter what their political persuasion. Sometimes, unfortunately, really good speeches are made after the television cameras and reporters have gone for the evening and the public never get to hear about them. But this is what he said in the economic debate, after Black Wednesday, which is so important I think it bears repeating.

'There is no doubt in my mind that this has been the biggest economic crisis for fifty years, since we were forced off the gold standard in 1941 for similar reasons, because we had committed our currency to an over-valuation through linking it to the gold standard. Winston Churchill, in his extreme old age, told me that he regarded his decision to link sterling to the gold standard as the biggest mistake that he had made in his life, bigger even than the Dardanelles, but he said that he did it on the advice of the governor of the Bank of England, all the leading bankers and experts and financial specialists. They all advised him to link sterling to the gold standard. That contributed to the appalling recession of the 1930s, which I am old enough to remember. One of my earliest memories as a boy is standing in the dole queue with my father. I remember the humiliation that he felt at being in that dole queue . . . I make no criticism of my Right Hon. Friends the Prime Minister and the Chancellor for repeatedly saying, in the weeks leading to the floating of the pound, that they would not in any circumstances allow it to float, realign or be devalued . . . *We* understand the reasons why this must be done, as do foreign exchange dealers and bankers, but the mass of ordinary people in this country do not. When political leaders make impassioned commitments and must then eat their own words a few weeks later, that is demeaning to the entire political process, and undermines the respect in which all constituents hold their Members of Parliament, irrespective of party.'

John Wilkinson arrived next. He is tall, straight, an ex-RAF officer and generally reserved, but fiery when he speaks on defence matters. He is bitterly opposed to the treaty because it requires us to sacrifice control of our defence to a group of bumbling incompetents in Brussels. How would we have fared in the last war if France or Belgium had been in charge of Europe's survival?

'Some freshmen are here,' I whispered to Chris Gill, as a group of them came through the door and seated themselves at the back of the room.

'Good. That's encouraging. If they've come to this meeting that probably means they'll stick with us.'

'Come in. Welcome,' Michael said again. 'I expect the

Whips have been giving you a rough time today. It's to be expected.'

'They frogmarched me onto the terrace for a bit of last-minute persuasion,' said Bernard Jenkin. The Whips, who considered Bernard part of the Establishment, probably thought he was a soft target. And he was getting flak from his constituency as well.

John Whittingdale, smiling as he always seems to do, came in looking every bit the new boy, anxious to please. But we were soon to learn that when he pleased he could change dramatically.

A tug-of-war had been going on between the pro- and anti-Maastricht factions for months but in the last few days it had hotted up. When Margaret Thatcher learned that some of the new members who owed their seats to her were wavering, she invited them to meet her in her room in the House of Lords. She had heard that John Whittingdale was thinking of abstaining. She reminded them of the importance of keeping our currency free from interference by a central-ized bank trying to rig exchange rates, and of what this would do to the economy. John knew this well: he had received his political spurs from her. Those who witnessed him emerging from the meeting described him as being 'ashen-faced and watery-eyed'. Later it was reported that she told him his spine did not appear to reach his brain.

Another of the new intakes was Iain Duncan-Smith, a young fogey, his brown trilby left over from his time as an army officer. Grey-haired, slightly balding but with a young face, he has bright attentive eyes which crinkle when he smiles. A lawyer, his grasp of the minutiae of the treaty helped to guide this younger group through the complex committee stage.

And Barry Legg. Taciturn, never wastes a word but is very determined. I knew him from my days on Westminster City Council when he was Chief Whip on the council. He never raised his voice but when he told you to do something it got done. This group sat together on the side chairs, away from the main table as if deferring to the older hands.

Vivian Bendall burst into the room. He's a long, gangling, Porsche-driving, right-winger, from the Essex constituency of Ilford North, known in the House as the taxi driver's friend: half of London's black-cab drivers live in his constituency.

'There is no way the Government is going to get me to vote for this treaty. I didn't come to this place to hand over the Government to a bunch of foreigners,' he announced with bravado. No one was going to push *him* into the arms of the Germans, he said. But he swooned like a lovestick maiden when the time came.

The room was getting crowded. James Cran and Christopher Gill sat together comparing notes, checking through their lists of possibles and probables. I looked around and wondered what motivated us all to be there. Were we Euro-rebels, Euro-phobes, Euro-sceptics? Or were we no-hopers, as the Prime Minister called us, or has-beens as the press alleged? If you have a House of Commons made up of people whose life's ambition is to be Minister for Drains, the House ceases to reflect the concerns of ordinary people. It was we, not the Government, who represented Joe Public's view. That was our vital function.

Besides, we knew from the polls and masses of letters we were getting that the public was on our side.

We had not come to this meeting to attack the Government. When Norman Fowler warned us we were playing with fire, Tony Marlow shot back, 'It's the Government that's playing with fire. If they carry on this way, they'll cause civil war within the party.'

And Nick Budgen chimed in with, 'We're shooting at the treaty, not Major. We hope he doesn't walk across our line of fire.'

For some people in the room, like Tony Marlow and Richard Shepherd, the debate over Maastricht was a battle of romantic nationalism. Some people in the room had a strong sense of their links with recent history and they felt they were fighting a battle similar to the one our parents fought in the Second World War. I remembered a recent lunch at the Caledonian Club when we met up with some of our supporters from the Lords.

'Your father was killed in the war. So was mine and so was Nick Budgen's,' said Bill Cash to Mickey (Lord) Suffolk whose father, a bomb disposal expert killed while defusing a bomb, was awarded the George Cross. Bill Cash's father, who was killed in action, was awarded the Military Cross. Bill appears to be a rather pedantic solicitor addicted to the minutiae of the treaty but has a strong sense of being part of tradition. His ancestors include John Bright, who campaigned in the nineteenth century for free trade and the abolition of the corn laws. Bill saw our battle in the same light as the Second World War: a battle for national integrity, which was threatened by Maastricht.

At the end of the table Michael sat, pen in hand, jotting down notes, ticking off names. He was a good chairman. Neither charismatic nor dominating, his natural good humour had kept us all together, so far. James Cran, Christopher Gill, Roger Knapman and I did the leg work and performed an equally important role. Our job was not to say much but to keep tabs on things.

'It's three minutes past starting time. More colleagues might come. But I think we can start.' I did a quick count. The buzz of conversation died down. 'The purpose of this meeting is to assess our chances tomorrow. It is time for us to commit ourselves. The Prime Minister has given us the best chance we'll ever get to kill this Bill before it kills us,' said Michael. 'I would like to get a commitment from all of you. But first I'll ask Bill Cash to state briefly why he thinks that if we can defeat the Government tomorrow the treaty is not just dead but also buried.'

Bill gave one of his polished briefings, explaining the intricacies of parliamentary procedure which would prevent the Prime Minister bringing the Bill back again in some other guise. As usual, he had taken the precaution of checking his view with those repositories of parliamentary procedure, the Clerks.

'Thanks, Bill,' said Michael. 'Now, will anyone who has decided to vote with the Government please leave the room.' We waited, tense, eyes moving around the gathering. I counted forty people now. A chair scraped. Someone got up and moved to the door. Then someone else, and another. They left silently, without resentment on our part. At least they were being honest.

'Now I want to go round the table to find out who will be voting No, and who will be abstaining.'

As each member stated his or her position, Christopher marked the names off on his list. So did Michael. 'Does that match up with your earlier calculations?' Michael asked. Christopher nodded. 'Then I think we're home and dry. So long as everyone remains committed. I ask you again: if you don't think you can go through with it please say so now. We don't want to be over-optimistic. But the numbers look satisfactory.'

It was our habit at these meetings not to declare what the numbers were. Some people just couldn't resist the temptation to pass on a piece of hot gossip. We were sure it would get back to the lobby correspondents, if not to the Whips directly.

Elsewhere in the building, government Whips were having their own meeting. They, too, were ticking off names on a list.

'These are the potential rebels,' said one of the Whips, indicating the board in their office. 'These are the ones we have converted, and these are still vulnerable. Go to work on them this evening and keep at them tomorrow.'

'What about the hard nuts? What should we do about those?'

'The usual. Tell them there'll be no promotion, no early nights, no foreign trips, no standing committee chairmanships. And no knighthood.'

Later that evening one of the new members who attended our meeting was frogmarched by a Whip to a dressing down on the chilly terrace.

'This rebellion will bring you ten minutes of fame and a lifetime in the political wilderness,' he was told. He caved in.

Bill Walker, the veteran Tory from Scotland, was threatened, unsuccessfully, with removal from the chairmanship of the backbench Scottish Affairs Committee.

A key player behind the scenes at Conservative Central Office was Sir Basil Feldman, chairman of the National Union, the party's voluntary wing. He sent a message to constituency chairmen explaining to them that the fate of the Government was at stake. Some members heard back from their chairmen in double quick time. Robin Hodgson, chairman of the West Midlands Central Council, shot off a letter to *The Times* that Bill Cash and Nick Budgen should be de-selected.

Christopher Gill telephoned Robin Hodgson. 'What about the other eight rebels in the area? Are you going to order a massacre?' he asked.

Next day, just before the debate opened, David Lightbown made a telephone call to Nicholas Budgen's association chairman, Rosanne Williams, who had already made it known that she disapproved of Nick's opposition.

Later she appeared on the main television news bulletins from a local station with Nick facing her from a London studio; they had a verbal punch-up watched by millions.

Walter Sweeney received a fax containing details of a motion passed by his constituency officers expressing displeasure at his intention of voting against the Government. Fifteen of the association had voted in favour of the motion, six against with four abstentions. It upset him.

Other people who attended our meeting that night were invited next day to meet John Major, Michael Heseltine or Richard Ryder, the Chief Whip, for a 'fireside chat'. And if that didn't work, another popular heavyweight Whip, Nicholas Soames, made it clear that the individual would sacrifice all hopes of a ministerial career.

The buzz of conversation in the room died down. 'Time for us to commit ourselves,' said Michael. The mood became serious. 'I don't know whether we're brave or stupid but I calculate we have enough people to win this vote. Not comfortably, but if everyone in this room sticks to what they have pledged in the last few minutes, the Maastricht treaty will be dead by ten o'clock tomorrow night.'

'We know we'll all be put under enormous pressure tomorrow. Perhaps it would be better to keep away from the House if you don't intend to speak in the debate or are going to abstain. If anyone is nervous or frightened, give me a call. Or Christopher, or Teresa. Let us know where you are and what you're up to and if you find out that any colleague is under particular pressure, we'll be there to stiffen their resolve.'

Bill Cash then intervened. 'Churchill said, "Your first duty is to your nation, your second is to your constituents. Only in the third instance do you have a duty to your party and its policies."'

We listened in silence.

'If we win tomorrow we will save the Government for Westminster. No greater challenge has ever faced a group of people in this House. Good luck,' said Michael.

The room began to clear and half a dozen of the inner core hung back in case there were any last-minute arrangements to be made.

'We will have to keep a close eye on some of them,' said Michael thoughtfully.

'There were thirty-two pledges altogether,' said Christopher Gill. 'We must expect a few of them to fall by the wayside but if we can hold on to twenty-six we're OK.'

'I had a word with Margaret today. She said she would be willing to talk to anyone whose backbone needs stiffening. She'll be available all day tomorrow in her room in the Lords. Let me know if you think there's anyone who needs to be sent along. I think she has already arranged to see the freshmen. And Norman [Tebbit] will be around the lobbies all day.'

'Sinking his teeth into the ankles of anyone he thinks might stray,' said Nicholas Winterton, quoting the Prime Minister's famous remark, made in the House after Black Wednesday.

'Or their trousers.'

We laughed.

15

INTO BATTLE

Norman Tebbit sat, like a cross between a vulture and an evangelist, on the green leather benches in the members' lobby, just outside the door leading to the Whips' corridor. From time to time wavering rebels were taken by our unofficial whips to meet him, so that he could have a little arm-twisting chat. He would hover there all afternoon and through to the early evening encouraging our weaker brethren to stick with their principles and take the opportunity provided by the paving debate to kill off the treaty.

Although he never attended any of our meetings – we were at pains to keep a distance between us and the older hands lest we should be accused of trying to jump on their bandwagon – he was, in his own way, extremely active. He was a great supporter of there being a referendum and spoke at a number of get-togethers with people who were organizing petitions for the public.

'If the people's answer is Yes to Maastricht at least it would have been their decision to give away control of their own affairs,' he told the *Independent*. 'This would leave the political system intact and, of particular interest one might have thought to the Prime Minister, leave the Tory party intact.' After a pause he added, 'You know, it might eventually occur to John Smith that a referendum would be the only way of leaving his party intact, too.' This, of course, was a reference to the fact that the Labour party had hoist itself with the same petard as the Tories.

For those who like to believe there is life after death, the anti-Maastricht campaign must have given them some hope – in the shape of Sir Edward Heath. Since losing the leadership to Margaret Thatcher in 1975, he had sat, grim and silent, across the aisle from the Chief Whip on the front bench. Now he was like a man who had been given a large dose of rejuvenating monkey glands. With the departure of Sir Bernard Brain as Leader of the House he now occupied that role which assured him of the Speaker's preference whenever he rose from his seat to speak. Over the weeks and months he certainly regained his voice.

Time and again he turned the screws on the anti-Maastricht group, a 'party within a party', as he labelled us. 'If they want an election on Maastricht they can form their own party,' he told *Channel 4 News*, adding that John Major should assert his authority by not being 'quite so nice' to the rebels. Decoded, the former prime minister's message to the current leader was that the time had come for a purge.

He walked past Norman muttering. 'This is absolutely appalling,' as he hurried to claim his regular corner seat. There is no love lost between Heath and Tebbit and he obviously considered the latter's lobbying of MPs like this bad form. As if he wouldn't stoop to doing anything so blatant himself if the need arose!

It was Wednesday 4 November and Question Time had just finished. Bowen Wells, MP for Hertford and Stortford, was introducing a ten-minute-rule Bill on the regulation of gypsy sites. The timing was unfortunate for him: most people coming into the chamber wanted to hear the Prime Minister open the paving debate and no one was paying him much attention. The rebels, the Whips and the Opposition had done their sums and, if people were to be relied upon, the Government could lose the vote at the end of the day.

By now the chamber was filled to overflowing and members were sitting in the aisles. There are 650 members of Parliament but there is room for only 470 of us on the benches so it is important to get in early if you want a seat. When Bowen Wells stood up formally to deliver his Bill into the hands of the Speaker, someone nipped in and pinched his seat. They're not all gentlemen in here.

The galleries above the chambers were packed – with MPs, the press, members of the public, and people from the Lords. Jeffrey Archer, now Lord Archer, was seated in the front of the strangers' gallery probably making mental notes for his next book.

Tension was running high when the Speaker, Betty Boothroyd, rose to open the debate. 'First, I want to tell the House that more than ninety Honourable Members have intimated to me they wish to speak in this debate. I therefore ask those who are called to exercise a great deal of restraint. I shall impose a ten-minute limit on speeches between the hours of six o'clock and eight o'clock. I selected the amendment in the name of the Leader of the Opposition so let us get on with it.'

No sooner had Betty sat down than pandemonium broke out as dozens of members leapt to their feet to make points of order. At last the House settled down and the Prime Minister rose to the dispatch box to open the debate.

The British Parliament is unique in its adversarial style. Unlike most, the two sides sit facing each other like rival football teams. But once play begins it is more like a cock-pit where the strutting opponents fight it out using arguments and insults instead of claws and beaks, although during the last few weeks many of us felt as if we had been pecked to death by the Whips.

I looked over at Bernard Jenkin and mouthed, 'Are you all right?' He nodded but grimaced. If the pressure on hard-liners like me was bad, on the new members like him it was intolerable. Deep Throat had clearly told the Whips we were in a position to defeat the Government and they had panicked. The gloves were off and the new boys were the Whips' prime targets. They needed to switch two of our members to be sure of winning. Every step that Bernard, Walter, Barry or Iain took around the building they were stopped by a member from one side or other, pressing them to vote with the Government or telling them to stick to their principles. Nor did the pressure end with face-to-face argu-ments. Their parliamentary offices were bombarded with calls from their constituencies, from both sides.

'Please, for God's sake, go with the Government,' one caller would say.

'Please, for God's sake, don't be pressurized into voting for this legislation,' the next one would plead.

Ann Jenkin, who runs Bernard's office, took dozens of calls over several days: by the day of the debate she had reached the end of her tether, having spent most of the night discussing the background with Bernard. Ann is as political as her husband. In 1987 they fought adjacent seats in Glasgow and both had long political pedigrees with the Conservative party. Bernard's father, Patrick Jenkin, was Secretary of State for the Environment before going to the House of Lords and he strongly disagreed with his son's views on Maastricht. Since both of them were close to their families the conversation hardly ever got away from the subject of politics.

That morning Ann arrived at her office, a few yards from mine, wearing no make-up and her face showing the strain of the phone calls she had fielded for the last seventy-two hours.

'You mustn't take any notice of the way I look. I shall probably be crying all day,' she told the two young male research assistants helping in her office.

She didn't have long to wait. Andrew Mitchell, a vice-chairman of the party, rang. 'Can't you do anything to make Bernard see sense?' he asked.

Ann could feel the tears rising. 'Bernard must make up his own mind—' She gulped. She couldn't finish the sentence.

Even though Andrew sensed the situation, he persisted. 'The party needs every vote and you both know enough about politics to realize the damage you will be doing.' Later, when he learned about this conversation Bernard was furious. It was one thing for the Whips to take it out on him; quite another to harangue his wife.

MPs are the jury of the nation: a mixed bag, sent there to keep an eye on the executive and see that it does not abuse its powers. We are certainly not there purely to toe the party line but to uphold the constitution which includes the right to be governed from Westminster, which is what the Euro-sceptics were fighting to retain during this paving debate. We believe no government has the right to transfer its power without first consulting the people in a general election or a referendum. But the general election of 1992 offered no choice: all three major parties were committed to take us deeper into Europe. It was something we felt passionate about, and feelings on all sides of the House were at fever pitch.

For weeks the Whips had been busy leaning on all the members who had signed Michael Spicer's two EDMs calling for a fresh start and there was no doubt their tactics brought some people into line. The latest rumour was that the Prime Minister had indicated he would call an election if he lost the vote. This was countered by another rumour that, on hearing this, Sir Norman Fowler went straight to the Prime Minister to tell him the party was in no shape to fight an election and that he, personally, would resign as party chairman if John Major made his threat official. How much truth there was in these rumours is anyone's guess but it certainly added to the drama of the occasion.

The Prime Minister was on his feet. '. . . duck, dodge or weave around the question . . . cast his principles adrift on a sea of expediency . . . the sort of contemptible wriggling that will earn no plaudits . . .' (The Prime Minister is always going on about wriggling. I wish he wouldn't. As a biologist I'm interested in worms but his repetition of the word 'wriggle' over and over again gives me the creeps. I wonder why he uses it so much?)

There was a lot of hollering and shouting going on and umpteen interruptions. He was giving way too much to members who wanted to intervene and he was losing his audience: people were getting restive.

Pugnacious Tony Marlow kept trying to get to his feet: he was talking about devils with horns and tails. I hadn't been paying attention and wondered if it was a reference to the Whips. Their behaviour had certainly been wicked.

At lunchtime I bumped into Walter Sweeney, who was

almost in tears after his run-in with the Chief Whip the day before. Walter is a solicitor who's as solid as a rock; very strong on law and order with what I would call old-fashioned Tory values, in the best sense. He had been subjected to considerable pressure from some people in his constituency which he had resisted. Then this morning he received a fax from the chairman of his association ordering him – *ordering*, mind – to vote with the Government.

'They are hinting that they will de-select me if I don't vote for the Government in the lobby tonight,' he said. He was visibly shaken. 'Apparently someone from Central Office has been down there to organize this.'

'You mean Central Office is leaning on party chairmen?' I was astounded.

'I believe so, yes,' he said, in his quiet, measured way. 'Other members have received similar "advice" in phone calls from their constituency offices.'

'It's absolutely outrageous. They should not be poking their nose in. Fowler must be behind this. It makes sense. The Prime Minister didn't make him chairman of the party for nothing. But you're fire-proof, Walter,' I went on. 'With a majority of nineteen they're not going to have a by-election. You'll have a battle to hold on to the seat, anyway, and you could make your reputation by sticking up for the independence of the country. Vote with your conscience not your career.'

Walter had already told me about his meeting with Richard Ryder, which he described as 'hitting below the belt'. 'It was very unpleasant and I did feel extremely emotional. Another Whip joked about breaking my kneecaps and blood on my shirt,' he added.

But Walter's torment did not end there. The following

day he received, anonymously in the post, an envelope containing a white feather. A most unfair comment by some cruel person which he didn't tell anyone about until our meeting the night before the social chapter debate, seven months later. He never found out whether it came from the government side or if it was from someone outside the House who had sent it to him for abstaining instead of voting against. After his experience during the paving debate, there was no question he would ever back off again, but it illustrates just how high feelings were running.

Bill Cash tried to get up to speak a few times while the Prime Minister was on his feet but he refused to give way: a speech by Bill was probably the last thing he wanted to hear then. But another backbencher was luckier. Sir Anthony Grant rose to plant one of those sycophantic interventions that make prime ministers preen and have the effect on the rest of us of making our toe nails curl: '. . . the Danish newspaper which asks, "Why is it that Major always gets his own way?" Can my Right Honourable Friend enlighten us on what appears to be an admirable performance by him?'

I couldn't stand this kind of stuff so decided to take a breather and bumped into Ann Jenkin in the corridor. There were two debates going on that day: one in the chamber under parliamentary rules of courtesy and decorum and another in the corridors, tea rooms and terraces where four-letter words, bribery and bitter insults were being traded between the Whips and the rebels. Every trick in the book, from threatening to expose who knows what scandal to intimating they could kiss goodbye to a knighthood, had been used by the Whips to bring people into line and they were still snarling and snapping at our heels while the debate was in progress.

However, although recently there had been some nasty goings on when hurtful things were said and done, the occasional shock-horror story turned out to be quite hilarious. There had been a newspaper headline which screamed: 'Whips tell MP's Sex Secrets.'

'Have you seen the *Sun* today?' one of Ann Jenkin's friends asked. 'The headline says "Whips Tell MP's Sex Secrets" and there's a photograph of Bernard with a caption, "Wife receives mystery phone call". What's going on?'

Ann felt her hair standing on end. 'You must be joking! Bernard hasn't any sex secrets. But he's always going round joking about sleeping with his beautiful secretary.'

There was a gasp at the other end of the line. 'Who's that?' asked the friend.

'Me, you idiot,' said Ann.

Ann told me she had had a phone call from James Arbuthnot, Bernard's Whip. It was another indication of just how desperate the Whips were getting.

'Ann, will you come and see me on the terrace?' he had asked. 'Just for a cup of tea and a chat. I'd love to see you.' Ann tried to contact Bernard to take his advice but couldn't find him. She knew James well, and liked him, and she felt that to refuse would be interpreted as a snub.

On the terrace, she spotted him standing by the wall overlooking the Thames. It only took a glance to see that James was almost as overwrought as she was herself. She knew that, as a free agent, he would broadly agree with Bernard's view but as a Whip he had the job of forcing people to do things against their conscience.

'You can't win, Ann. If the Government loses the Prime Minister will resign,' he said.

'That's nonsense. All he needs is to call a vote of

confidence the day after and his position will be secured. I can't bear to wake up tomorrow morning and hear the *Today* programme crowing that the Fresh Start group has been beaten. It would be a travesty after everything they've gone through. And Bernard really believes the Maastricht treaty is terrible. So do I, for that matter,' she said.

'I promise you, I really do understand what you are going through. It isn't too easy for me either.' He paused. 'I'll never ever go through this again,' he said firmly. 'I don't want to be party to anything like this ever again.'

I put my hand on Ann's arm and gave her a squeeze. We needed to support each other. As I made my way to the tea room, little did I know just how much support I would be needing myself before the debate was over.

That evening, Ann told me later, she had tickets for a concert at the Barbican and said to Bernard. 'Why don't you come with me and get away from it all?' By then, he had decided to abstain in the vote instead of voting against the Government. There was no real reason why he should remain in the Commons, but he felt his absence would be construed as cowardice.

'You go. I'll find somewhere out of the firing line whilst the vote is going on,' he told her.

As tension built up, nowhere was safe: the Whips were everywhere – even in the lavatories. A story was sweeping Westminster that when it came time for the vote, heavy-weight Whip David Lightbown, who has a walk like a bull elephant – his head and body roll into the room ahead of the rest of him – trapped a luckless Euro-rebel in the lavatory. He wanted to catch him to give him a dressing down, and where else to do so than the place where so much of our parliamentary business is conducted? Whoever Lightbown's quarry was, the manoeuvre didn't do him much good because while he was busy throwing his weight about he somehow got stuck in the john and missed the vote altogether!

As ten o'clock approached and tension mounted, Bernard paused in Central Lobby to talk to some visitors waiting to see their MP. He glanced towards the corridor leading to the Lords. Maybe his father was in there right now. And then he realized: the corridor, lined with leather benches, was completely deserted, perhaps the only empty place in the House. He walked slowly along it, looking at the murals which lined the walls. The first one showed Speaker Lenthall challenging the soldiers who came to arrest MPs who had refused to bow to the King's demand for more taxes. The beginning of the civil war. Bernard smiled. Tonight's battle was not the first time the British people had fought to retain the right to govern themselves. Perhaps we needed another Cromwell. Perhaps we had one in Margaret Thatcher or Norman Tebbit. We certainly had more people in the Fresh Start group than Lenthall had mustered in the picture. Big Ben chimed ten o'clock. The policeman in Central Lobby yelled, 'Division!' and the division bell began to ring loudly. Bernard sat down and rested his head against the wall. In fifteen to twenty minutes it would all be over, he thought, as members started scuttling through Central Lobby on their way to vote.

16

DIRTY
TACTICS

Sometime during that day an MP, who shall be name-
less, accosted me demanding to know why I wasn't
supporting the Government. He normally doesn't
talk to me and when he does has the irritating habit of
making silly sexist remarks. I've no idea why. Shoving his
face aggressively close to mine, he told me how I should be
answerable for my disloyalty.

I brushed him aside. 'You have to live with your own
conscience and I have to live with mine,' I told him. 'I can
make up my own mind and don't need help from you.'

When I went back to listen to the debate I sat on one
of the few spare seats next to another MP who I shall not
name.

After a short time, I realized that the MP who had
accosted me in the corridor had sat next to me. The two of
them immediately began to banter between them. One said
something like, 'You know she's talking about voting against
the Government?'

The other one said, 'I always said we shouldn't let women
in here in the first place. They're a thundering nuisance.'

I realized they were trying to provoke me but it was a
bait I wasn't going to rise to.

Then the first said, 'A woman's place is in the home.'

'Yes, flat on her back.'

I felt trapped. I didn't want to get up and leave. Why

should I? On the other hand, I didn't just want to sit there as if I didn't mind. I sat, my back pressed hard against the wooden seat, staring ahead, my mind racing, wondering what to do. Should I get up and leave? Should I say something? But that would give them the satisfaction of thinking they had got to me. The conversation continued. It got worse.

One of them said, 'Do you think Teresa would be any good on her back? I wonder what kind of knickers she wears.' What he went on to say, I cannot bring myself to repeat here, but I could no longer put up with it. I exploded. 'Why don't you go somewhere else and find someone else to talk dirty to if you feel like that?'

'I thought you'd be enjoying it. I thought that's what you liked about this place, plenty of men.'

I felt angry and humiliated. They were obviously enjoying themselves because they were upsetting me.

'Women should be barefoot and pregnant. They shouldn't be let in here in the first place.'

I said angrily, 'Margaret ran rings round most of the men in this place.'

'That old cow,' said the one on my left, whose hatred for Margaret Thatcher corresponded with the rise of John Major. 'She would have lost us the last election, stupid bitch.'

I wasn't quite sure why they were saying this unless it was because they knew I was a fan of hers.

'John Major is bloody marvellous. He won us the election. And you're trying to undermine him,' he spat out.

'I'm trying to make sure there's still a purpose to our being here. If we don't defeat this treaty we may as well pack up and go home. We're turkeys voting for Christmas. It

won't be long before the public twigs and we get our P.45s,'
I said.

In the end I did get up, hurried down the centre aisle
and out of the chamber. It was the worst half-hour I think I
have spent in all my life; nothing quite like it has ever
happened to me before. I thought of all the times I had read
about young women complaining of this sort of thing. Now
I'd experienced the way it makes you feel: as if someone had
smeared dirt over you.

How dare they? I thought. What to do next? I felt myself
shaking. I looked around for my Whip, but there was hardly
anyone in the lobby. I spotted a couple of the women lobby
correspondents and half felt like unburdening myself to
them. Of course I couldn't tell them. It would have been in
the newspapers next day. The *Today* correspondent came up
to me. 'What's it like in the chamber?' he asked.

'I suppose it depends on what sex you are. I've just been
given what I believe is commonly known as a going-over. I
think it's also called sexual harassment.'

'Christ,' he said. 'Why don't you tell me about it?' I knew
already I'd said too much. 'No details, and this is on lobby
terms,' I said, turning on my heel.

I made my way into the members' post office off the
lobby. In there, there are always supplies of writing paper
and envelopes. I took a piece from the rack.

Banter between members is acceptable [I
wrote], but what you were doing tonight in the
chamber was talking dirty which is quite
unacceptable. Please don't come and sit near me
again. Teresa.

I put it in an envelope, to send to the one who was particularly offensive, then took it across to the members' letter board. He'd get it as soon as he came out of the chamber. I hoped it would have the same effect on him as his words had had on me. I thought that was preferable to a public demonstration of me slapping his face. That would have been so embarrassing in the chamber in front of the television cameras, the gallery full of press correspondents and members of the public.

It was a deliberate attempt to try to upset me. When I reported to my Whip that the two men had been extremely vulgar, he said he'd have a word with them. Since then, the first has stormed past me with his head down. It has created an unpleasant tension between us, which is a pity because before that he had been perfectly pleasant. I even went to his constituency once and talked to his women's group at his request as I so often do for colleagues in the House.

I have been instructed by lawyers to remove anything which will identify either of these MPs. I have no doubt I would win a court case but because of our ludicrous libel laws just by instigating proceedings they could have prevented publication of this book. Publication is more important to me than showing them up for the vermin they are, though I hope they will recognize themselves and that they are now thoroughly ashamed of their conduct. They ought to be.

When I went out on to the terrace to get a breath of air before going back into the chamber, John Taylor, the Ulster Unionist, was saying what an excellent debate it had been. (The Ulster Unionists were the staunchest anti-Europeans and had said so in their election manifesto.) 'There was only one sour note,' he said, 'which unfortunately came from Sir

Edward Heath, in his offensive and arrogant personal attack on John Smith. At one stage, I had to check that the new Leader of the Opposition was not a woman, such was the vigour of Heath's personal attack.'

I laughed and felt the tension ease a little.

Michael Carttiss, who had indicated to us the night before that he would vote against the Government, vowed in his speech, 'I shall vote . . . for a referendum so that the people of this country can decide.' Great, terrific, I thought.

Yet when it was time to go into the division lobby he was ambushed by the Prime Minister, who put his arm round Michael's shoulder and physically conducted him into the government lobby telling him, 'Michael, we could lose . . .'

'I was not going to be responsible for his downfall,' Michael said later. Big deal.

Then suddenly it was all over. Douglas Hurd was at the dispatch box, his eyes glued to the digital clock in front of him, racing through his winding-up remarks, and was pulled down into his seat by the Chief Whip. Betty, her eyes fixed on the clock opposite her at the far end of the chamber, rose to her feet. Outside Big Ben chimed ten o'clock but such was the noise that it couldn't be heard.

'. . . the question now being put . . .' Betty yelled, and she repeated the motion. 'Ayes to the right, noes to the left,' she yelled again. Policemen all around the Commons yelled, 'Division!' The division bell began to ring in the House, in restaurants where MPs gather in the evening, in members' homes. Bleepers began to bleep and from ministries around Whitehall, ministers and secretaries of state made for their chauffeur-driven cars which would whisk them back to the Commons. As far away as Park Lane in the West End members attending functions made a dash for the front lobby and a taxi to get back to the House within the eight minutes allowed for them to present themselves and be counted. The chamber, which a few minutes earlier had been a seated mass of humanity, began to get to its feet, like a theatre when a show is over and the lights go up. Slowly, MPs shuffled towards whichever lobby they were voting in.

Voting against your own side is like swimming upstream through a shoal of piranhas. I battled to cross the chamber through the throng going in the opposite direction and felt quite a number of elbows deliberately poked into my ribs. Some bump into you accidentally, some on purpose.

Others mutter.

'Scab!'

'Judas!' I was asked if I had been given thirty pieces of silver for my disloyalty.

'Don't do it, Teresa.'

Some tugged at my clothing. 'Come this way with us. This is where you belong.'

Still others said, 'No, she doesn't. She ought to be over there with that lot,' indicating the Labour party.

It was true, I was voting in the lobby with Labour, though not because I agreed with them. On the contrary, it was the only way for us to express our opposition to the treaty.

I kept my eyes down and made for the nearest door in the 'No' lobby. It felt completely alien. I spotted Ann Winterton and moved quickly to her side. 'Shall we go through together?'

'Yes, let's,' she said. 'Less hassle.'

We were greeted with cat-calls and some ribaldry. 'What are you doing in here, Teresa?'

'Changing sides? Have you decided to join the Labour party?'

'Have you decided to dump them after all?'

There was a lot of laughter.

I managed a watery smile. I felt as out of place as a nun in a bordello.

As colleagues streamed out of the lobbies a posse of frontbench ministers including Michael Heseltine surrounded Sir Ivan Lawrence, but he is a seasoned campaigner and sat on his hands. He was not going to be intimidated, even by the heavy mob. He nonchalantly resisted their blandishments as they argued ferociously with him. He had already warned the Prime Minister on the BBC's breakfast-time news programme, 'We want you to stay, but do not push us beyond the realms of endurance.'

It was a tactical mistake to be dotted all over the chamber and there was no question that the government Whips knew exactly who were the most vulnerable, who they had to go for in a last-minute bid to secure this cliff-hanger of a vote. We should have sat together: there's strength in numbers.

If anyone thinks you enjoy being a rebel they can never have experienced it. You go reluctantly, conscious that you are moving in an alien environment, surrounded by faces you normally only see from a distance across the House.

We shuffled past a clerk at the end of the lobby who sits at a high oak desk like someone in a Dickensian counting house. 'Gorman,' I shouted as I went by; he ticked off the name on his list.

'Winterton,' called Ann. Moving past him, we reached the exit, paused, bowed to the tellers on the other side of the door, then walked through.

This allows the Whips to count the numbers voting. The

government Whip stared at us coldly, reprimanding us without words. I spotted Christopher Gill checking our supporters. 'How are we doing?' I asked him.

'Not too bad,' he replied. But he looked nervous. Tonight, when the vote was critical, the group hanging around outside the voting lobby was larger than usual and fighting your way through it to get back into the chamber was no mean task.

'Close the doors!' yelled the Speaker, as the clock ticked eight minutes past the hour.

'Close the doors!' echoed the doormen, posted at the entrance to each voting lobby and on the two doors which lead into it from the back of the chamber. Inside the lobby, members continued to shuffle through. Some lingered on the side benches, chatting. Eventually a Whip brought up the rear, ushering people through, keeping them moving.

'All out!' shouted the Whip from inside the lobby.

The tellers on the door compared notes. Then, turning towards the chamber, they hurried in to meet their counterparts from the other lobby. The four of them lined up, facing the Speaker.

'Order!' shouted Betty, and in an instant the House was silent. People scrambled for a seat to clear a way for the tellers to move forward. Five long paces to the edge of the table. The four nod in unison.

'The ayes to the right three hundred and sixteen, the noes to the left three hundred and thirteen, so the ayes have it,' Betty yelled.

Uproar broke out. The Government had won by three votes. People were on their feet, Tories cheering, waving their order papers, the Labour members shaking their heads, taunting the Tory benches over such a close shave.

MPs pushed their way out, hurrying across to the green outside where the media gather, anxious to give their reaction to the waiting listeners and viewers. Groups of Eurosceptics who had pinned their hopes on this vote stood in the members' lobby. Some were despondent, others very angry.

'How the hell could Michael Carttiss have voted in the Government lobby when half an hour before he told the House in his speech he wasn't going to?'

'The Prime Minister put his arm round him and he melted like a snowball in hell.'

'And Robert Jones?'

'He voted with the Government.'

'John Smith's speech made him change his mind!'

'Bullshit.'

'Vivian Bendall?'

'He ratted on us, too.'

'We must learn some lessons. Some of our people were nobbled in the chamber at the last minute.'

'We could have prevented that if we had all sat together in a group,' I said.

'What gets me is they gave their word. Why didn't they say yesterday if they hadn't the bottle to go through with it?' James Cran's voice was bitter.

I spotted Walter Sweeney on his way out of the lobby, and moved quickly after him. 'You were brave, Walter. I know it wasn't easy for you.'

Walter smiled. 'Brave or stupid,' he said.

'Don't blame yourself. You did the right thing. You're braver than all those Tories who know the treaty is wrong but voted for it anyway. You keep your integrity. That's honourable. Your constituents will respect you for it. You'll see.'

'Have you a list of those who rebelled?' asked the lobby correspondents, buzzing around us.

'How many abstained and how many voted against?'

'How did you vote, Teresa?'

The lobby correspondents have to work quickly to meet a deadline for the late-night editions of their newspapers, held over for the vote.

'Shall we meet afterwards for a drink at Rodin's?' suggested James Cran.

'Yes, let's. Will Michael come? And I'll try to find Roger. Let's meet here in ten minutes and go across together.'

As we left the Commons and crossed the road, Abingdon Green with its great Henry Moore statue was lit up like a fairground. All the major television channels were out there, spotlights blazing, microphones in hand. Well-known political commentators stood, backs to the cameras, each questioning an MP, who was blinking in the light. I spotted Bill Cash, Teddy Taylor, Nick Budgen, Tony Benn, Bryan Gould. And some of the Euro-fanatics.

'Delighted.'

'Disappointed.'

'A great night for the Prime Minister,' one said.

'A sad day for the country,' said someone else.

The comments came thick and fast: predictable, angry. Everyone determined to put a brave face on it.

Later, in Rodin's, we went over the day's events.

'We should have won it.'

'We could have.'

'We have to learn from this. Now we'll have to fight the whole thing through to the bitter end.'

'Yes, but we still have plenty of opportunities to win. We're not beaten yet.'

17

THE MALE
MENOPAUSE

Battles in Parliament are fought with arguments in the
chamber of the House. The committee stage of any
Bill is not usually much of an attention grabber: it
is the time when the fine print of the legislation is picked
over in detail. It requires the kind of dedication shown by a
swot who is determined to get an A grade in an exam. Since
the future liberty of the British people was at stake with this
treaty, it is just as well some people on the back-benches had
the wit and the patience to do it. Champion nit-pickers are
Sir Teddy Taylor and Bill Cash. I am a sloth. I find the text a
bit like the maze at Hampton Court: when I tried to find my
way through I got completely lost. Thank goodness a
number of our colleagues had more patience.

Except for lobby correspondents and television pro-
ducers, for whom this kind of discussion is meat and drink,
Parliament's committee meetings are a bit of a turn-off. Most
are held in one of the rooms on the upper floors and,
although open to the public, very few outsiders turn up. But
this one was different. It was held in the chamber and
presided over by one of the deputy speakers. The Mace,
symbol of the Commons in session, was relegated to its
cradle below the front table.

Thanks to television, the layout of the chamber is familiar
to most people, but the feel of it isn't. It's like a theatre –
perhaps that's why no one seems to behave normally once

they get inside; everyone puts on an act from the Prime Minister down. Experienced parliamentarians tremble when they deliver their lines. Some, who are as mild as milk outside the chamber, become belligerent and aggressive once they reach the green leather benches. Others, like Dennis Skinner, hold the attention of the audience with one-liners and tall stories, while Michael Heseltine can pack the House from the front stall to the gallery.

All performances are closely monitored by the Whip, crouched on the front bench, scribbling in a little black book. Notes like 'Teresa Gorman made a helpful [or unhelpful] intervention.' Of such records are careers made or broken. By the end of the Maastricht battle I imagine most Euro-rebels had used up all their previously earned Brownie points.

Someone viewing the proceedings from the gallery or on television would hardly notice the difference from a usual parliamentary debate, though anyone taking a keen interest might have wondered why so few MPs from the ruling party appeared to speak in support of their government. That is because they were under strict orders from the Whips not to do so. The Government's objective was to get the legislation through as quickly as possible; the role of the opposition was to slow it down. In this case we were in the unusual position of being in opposition while the Labour party was at one with the Government. The only real difference was that the Labour party wanted the social chapter back in.

With both battalions ranged against us, we had to find a way of breaking through their wall of apparent solidarity, discover a weak spot where the Labour party was unlikely to vote with the Government, then try to set up some kind of a deal to bring their shaky alliance tumbling down. During all the time the Maastricht Bill was being considered, the

Government was able to rely on the support of the Liberal Democrats whose numbers, twenty-two, cancelled us out. Everything turned on the votes of the Ulster Unionists. They had trumpeted their opposition to Maastricht in their election manifesto so were happy to join us in trying to defeat the wretched thing.

The deputy speaker, Michael Morris, who looks like a toby jug, was in charge. There was a lot of controversy about how he handled his job and he was offended at the censure motion from Tony Benn that implied he wasn't doing it properly, which, of course, was rejected. At Westminster we pride ourselves on the fair and objective way we conduct debates and to acknowledge that the chairman of a committee is capable of favouring one side or the other would make the House of Commons look like a third-world republic, or even Italy.

Before the debate proper could get going, there were a lot of procedural knots to untie. One of them got a rise out of Dennis Skinner.

During the debate on Benn's motion, Dennis, always exasperated by tortuous procedural gobbledegook, asked, 'Isn't it time we stopped this nonsense of saying the chair cannot explain why he has made a decision to discuss, or not, an issue? We are approaching the twenty-first century and a leading member of the House of Commons is not able to tell the assembled members, "The reason why I am not selecting your amendment or putting it to the vote is the following." What is it all for?' It was in this speech that Dennis made his famous remark about Margaret Thatcher, 'They chucked her out like a dog in the night.'

I agreed with him about that and I agreed with him about what was and what was not being allowed to be debated. Perhaps I sound harsh, but his decisions were incredibly frustrating for us, especially when we passionately wanted to speak. I get frustrated with so many of the anachronisms which dominate the parliamentary process and which can twist and pervert the way I believe it ought to go

Take knighthoods (not of course suggesting for a moment that Michael Morris had this in mind during the debate). I would abolish them tomorrow and I can't understand why John Major doesn't. How will he ever get his classless society if he keeps perpetuating such an archaic system?

Once, when Nicholas Winterton made an impassioned speech about the textile industry, Cyril Smith shouted across the chamber, 'Nick, your knighthood is disappearing but your peerage is imminent.' Nick replied, 'If I were a lord, I would call myself Lord Winterton of Winkle!' They all pretend they have no interest whatsoever in being ennobled – but don't you believe it. Sir Ivan Lawrence, whose Euro-rebel credentials are impeccable, is inordinately proud of his 'Sir' although, like most of them, he insists he accepted it more for his wife's benefit than his own.

I wonder, how can they sell their souls? I asked Michael Spicer, 'Why does it matter so much to you boys?'

And he told me, 'Well, Teresa, it's like a male menopause. We know it's all downhill from now on, so it's a consolation prize. It's also a reward for the wife after years of hanging around at home never knowing if her husband's coming back and having to spend time going to other people's coffee mornings.'

I think it is the ultimate seduction. Before the general election, Teddy Taylor was momentarily seduced like that. He voted with the Government just before John Major went off to Maastricht and soon afterwards got a knighthood. He felt so bad about it that he went to Michael Spicer and said, 'I don't know if I can go on with my battle now I've taken the Queen's shilling.'

But Michael assured him he could make up for it and I must say he has tried to make amends for having ratted.

What would happen, I wonder, if an MP had this particular carrot dangled in front of him and the Prime Minister welshed on his promise? I suppose there must be honour among thieves.

In the committee stage we had to try to win one of the votes at the end of the day's debate.

As 'whip' on duty in the chamber, it was my job to stay to the bitter end, sitting it out on the benches. Several times the Government forced the debate to keep going through the night. It was part of their strategy to wear us down. That's not too bad until one or two in the morning. Then, the glowing lights in the chamber, extra bright to suit the television cameras, begin to burn into your eyes, making them feel sore and eventually close.

Between two and three it's a real battle to keep awake. Four to five often passes quickly, as you nod off, except for when the chairman calls a halt to a part of the debate and the division bell rings. Then people come scuttling from their sleeping holes. It isn't until you've been through one of these late-night sittings that you realize the purpose of the large green leather armchairs dotted all over the place. MPs come from everywhere, bleary-eyed, unsteady on their feet, somnambulant and silent, shuffling zombie-like. Just before dawn the Whips call a halt.

You stagger into the fresh air and walk unsteadily across the road, the cold wind coming off the Thames pinching your cheeks. Grey skies, a few cars, a few early workers about – it's like being in another world. You creep in, trying not to wake the household, which is usually sound asleep. Cold and exhausted, you slip between the sheets and snuggle up to the warm body in the bed beside you.

'What time is it?' the body mutters from deep inside the world of sleep.

'It's six in the morning. Go back to sleep. And don't wake me when you get up.'

Sometimes, when sleep overcame me, I stretched out on the side benches beneath the gallery, hoping the cameras couldn't see me. This is a risky strategy: if your mouth falls open and you snore, the microphones will record the noise for posterity. If this happens, a kindly colleague will usually come across and shake you. In the small hours of the morning, even frontbench spokesmen are inclined to nod off. The whole mad business is no way to run a country, or debate an issue on which the future of our democracy depends.

18

THE BULLDOG BREED

Those opposed to a Bill table amendments to it. The chairman chooses which ones will be debated but his selection need only be announced one day before, which is why we had to practise some fairly fast footwork.

Teddy Taylor and Bill Cash between them were the most assiduous attenders. They tabled hundreds of amendments with the clear intention of keeping the debate going as long as possible: the more it was exposed to public view, the more its shortcomings were recognized. They knew their stuff backwards and could always be relied upon to make a solid speech as they could talk for an hour or more on the most obscure details – and sometimes did. Bill was accused of filibustering on more than one occasion by being on his feet for longer than an hour.

Teddy Taylor once asked me to go and talk to his ladies' group at a lunch and, I have to say, driving to Southend in the middle of the day is not something I would choose to do, but I absolutely love him and I'd do anything for him. It was a very odd journey: he is famous for being a teetotaller but he smokes like a chimney in the car – his wife, Sheila, disapproves of him smoking. And it is a car which seems to need more petrol than most but I soon twigged the reason: he's a secret sweet-eater. Every time he stops for petrol he comes back with a handful of Wispa bars.

Like all of us, Sir Teddy had no illusions about the size of our struggle. Never mind convincing the public, just getting colleagues to get their brains round the Bill was an uphill task. After one debate, he told me, 'The saddest aspect is the way the majority of MPs seem to switch off and avoid listening to the arguments. Just after I had made one of my most telling and thought-provoking speeches, in my opinion, one of my Essex colleagues came up to me with a simple request: "I am not really interested at all in all this sovereignty business, I just want to know when you chaps are going to belt up and let me get to bed!" I think it was probably one of the most honest comments from a Europhile in the whole debate.'

The Maastricht debate threw up some of the best speeches I have ever listened to in the House. All through the public rooms and inside everyone's office is a television monitor which tells you who is currently speaking in the chamber. Big names send people scurrying to listen. As it happens, many of the best speeches are made by people whose names are little known and who are called long after the time when most sensible people have gone to bed. Luckily you can always read what they had to say next day in Hansard or, nowadays, get a video of the speech. I am sure that future generations of young people doing research on Parliament will discover and marvel at them.

Two of the best speakers are Richard Shepherd, who makes fiery, patriotic speeches, like Kenneth Branagh on a good day, and Sir Peter Tapsell. My favourite was delivered by Sir Peter, who had his arm twisted by Michael Heseltine. Since Peter was one of Hezza's sponsors for the leadership, the President of the Board of Trade presumably felt he could be leaned on. He was told to come back into the government fold, it would be better for his career prospects, which is rather a sick joke, really.

At the age of sixty-three I think he's past succumbing to ministerial blandishments. Peter summed up his feelings in a stirring speech: 'I remember,' he said, 'Walter Elliott, who was Minister of Agriculture here in the 1930s and who had voted for the Munich Agreement, telling me that he had done so out of a sense of personal loyalty to Neville Chamberlain. He said he admired Chamberlain as a man and felt he had done a good job domestically. Walter Elliott said that voting for Munich had not only eventually wrecked his own political career but, more importantly, had damaged his self-esteem. He said he had never ceased to reproach himself for that vote as events unfolded.

'I ask my younger friends who have not been in this House very long but who know in their hearts that the Maastricht treaty is not right for Britain to remember Walker Elliott.

'When I became an MP thirty-four years ago there were still a lot of Conservative members who had sat in the chamber through all the debates on Chamberlain's appeasement policy. But I never spoke to one of them who could recall ever having supported it. I sometimes used to wonder whether the Munich Agreement was carried through the House single-handed by Neville Chamberlain and the Conservative Whips' office. I predict that, ten years from now, there will be very few Tory Members of Parliament who will find it easy to recall they were ever supporters of the treaty.

'People should not be under the illusion that a central bank will show a degree of political independence when faced with ruthless and corrupt politicians. Under the Maastricht treaty no effective accountability will exist or could exist. The Reichsbank, the predecessor to the Bundesbank, became Hitler's creature and provided him with the sinews of war. If we lose control over our currency the House will lose the rock on which our democracy is founded – control over the money supply. Our constituents will effectively be disenfranchised. We will effectively be echoing Cromwell's words when he pointed to the Mace and said, "Take that bauble away."

'I am rather bored with ministers, retired ambassadors and grandees in the City taking me on one side and saying in a patronizing way, "Can't you be a little more sophisticated in your approach to this treaty? We all understand it is a nonsense. It is absolutely unworkable. It will never take effect. But, my boy" – I am getting somewhat elderly to be addressed in that way but that is the tone of voice – "if we vote against the Maastricht treaty we shall lose all our influence in Europe. Therefore you must vote for this ludicrous and unworkable treaty. Don't let's worry about the wording of it." That is the advice they give me.'

When Kenneth Clarke remarked during the course of these debates, 'You can't have twenty, thirty or forty Euro-rebels determining the government of this country. They cannot be the tail that wags the dog', he didn't mention that it is because rebels like Sir Peter have a better pedigree, of the good old British bulldog sort, that they regard it as their duty to defend the country from government poodles.

I'm not the only one impressed with Peter's speech, of which I have quoted only a brief passage. He received a warm letter from Vernon Bogdanor, Reader in Government at Oxford, who said, 'I must express my admiration for your masterly speech in the committee stage of the European Communities (Amendment) Bill. I do not think that I have ever seen the case against a European central bank put so cogently.'

Tony Marlow, Michael Spicer, Nicholas Budgen, Nicholas Winterton, Richard Shepherd and Dick Body were also regular attenders questioning the minister, interrupting with points of order. Tristan Garel-Jones, the minister in charge, would loll on the front bench, feet up on the table in front, acting the part of someone bored to death with the whole proceedings. One evening when the debate was finished I asked him why he hadn't answered a question put to him by Christopher Gill.

'I never bother with questions from people who are totally opposed to the Bill,' he replied at his supercilious best. 'I just wish you would get off my back.'

'That's what we're here for, to get on the backs of cynics like you.' I was so angry. He waved me away and beetled off towards the Whips' office.

For my part I sat through all twenty-two days of it, keeping an eagle eye on our numbers.

It was a mark of the discipline and good humour of our group that my colleagues rarely demurred when I asked them to be in the chamber, even when this meant that they had to hurry back to London from a constituency engagement. I was impressed. My experience as a Whip on Westminster City Council for four years had not prepared me for such cooperation. Some members of the group seemed so grand I half expected them to brush aside my requests. Not a bit of it. Years of discipline by the official Whips had ingrained in them a respect for the office I held, even though it was unofficial. Chief Whip Richard Ryder would have been proud of me, even though I doubt he will ever offer me a job!

Everything we were doing was psychological warfare: the Government loses face if any part of its legislation is defeated. If we had achieved a victory, any change would have meant renegotiating the treaty. These were the bullets and bombs with which we fought our battles to retain democracy in Westminster. It may all appear dull and pedantic to the layman but we were fighting for all our futures. Even these weapons can, on occasion, produce some pretty dramatic explosions. Most of those were centred around the social chapter of which more later.

Despite long and boring stretches there were also some spectacularly exciting moments for us, such as when committee chairman Michael Morris was challenged over his judgement by Tony Benn, and the time when we discovered a chink in the Government's armour over an obscure item in the legislation about setting up a committee of the regions. We won a vote on that but the Government conceded our victory next day and avoided a confrontation.

The detail hardly matters: the emotional effect on us and the Government when it lost the vote was crucial. On an occasion like that, after the House closed down for the evening, we all trooped off to the bar for a celebratory drink. I suppose it must have felt something like that during the war when you managed to knock out a couple of the enemy's guns.

But anyone who thinks voting against your own side is easy has never been part of a team. The captain's word is law unless you disagree so fundamentally you can summon up the courage from somewhere to flout his commands, as in *Mutiny on the Bounty*. I still haven't developed skin thick enough to carry it off without suffering from butterflies in the stomach.

One evening I went back into the chamber late to vote and was standing alongside the Speaker's chair. I joined the line shuffling up the aisle towards the entrance at the back which leads to the division lobby. The door was open, guarded by a doorman waiting to slam it shut when Betty yelled, 'Close the doors!' after the eight minutes were up. (Sometimes members rushing to get through the door before it closes have punch-ups with the doorman: it's better not to leave it until the last minute.) On the other side of the entrance is a small platform from which a short flight of stairs leads down into the voting lobby. I stepped on to this platform and paused for a moment to peer through the bars of a wooden grille at the members now filling the lobby, looking around to see whether any of my chums were in sight. As my glance swept across their heads, there was the Prime Minister glancing up at me. We made instant eye contact: I didn't know whether to smile, stare blankly or look away. I felt like a schoolgirl caught out playing truant; for the last two evenings I had been voting against the Government on the Maastricht Bill. I hesitated; the Prime Minister raised his arms towards me like a shepherd welcoming a black sheep back to the fold. I was already walking down the stairs, my brain frantically casting around for what he could say to me.

'You were fabulous on television the other day,' he said. 'You really cheered me up – and Norma.' He was referring to an interview I had given to Sky Television when the unpleasant business about Clare Latimer and the *New Statesman* came out. I had said that I hoped the Prime Minister would stand up to them and kick them in the goolies. The news item was re-broadcast on CNN news and was seen by the Prime Minister on his stopover in Riyadh where he was selling planes to the Saudis. I also sent him and Clare Latimer a card to cheer them up, and he, in his turn, had sent me a thank-you note.

'Thank you for your letter,' I said to him. 'It cheered my office up no end. It's hard on them, too, to work for an MP who's losing all her Brownie points with the Whips and the Government,' I joked.

The Prime Minister took my hand in his. 'Come and sit down here on the bench and tell me why you're so worried about this treaty. You don't have to be, you know.' He led me through the crush to the benches. We sat facing each other. I could feel the eyes of some of the old tufton-buftons as they passed, some no doubt hoping the Prime Minister was giving me a ticking off, others probably jealous he should waste any time with me.

John patted my hand. 'You don't have to lose your Brownie points. You could drop this opposition and trust me to do what's best for the country.' He still had my hand between his. It was very seductive: I could feel myself tingling all over.

'I really would prefer to be on your side,' I heard myself saying feebly. 'Once it's all over I promise you I will never vote against the Government again.'

He chuckled. 'Is that a promise?' he asked me, still not letting go of my hand.

'Well, I wouldn't rely on it, but I'll do my very best.'

This is what it must feel like to be a convert at a Billy Graham revivalist meeting, I thought. I genuinely wanted to please the Prime Minister. It's a rotten job, and although I completely disagree with him on Europe, as a human being

I can't help responding to him. But I am not about to give up my old-fashioned faith in Britain for the new-fangled European religion.

After the Bill finished its committee stage it went to the House of Lords for examination. There, led by Lord Blake, the Lords tried to introduce an amendment which would force the Government to hold a referendum. Faced with the threat of the Lords altering the Bill, the Whips again got busy and raked out all the old tufton-buftons from the shires. The result: the Government majority of 269, which goes to show how you can overturn the democratic process when you have an unelected upper house.

After the Lords, a Bill comes back to the House of Commons for its third reading and any amendments made by the Lords are re-examined in the Commons – and usually thrown out again. When the House of Commons voted at the end of this debate, forty-one Conservative MPs rebelled against the Government. Normally, this would be a very serious matter indeed for a party in power but on this occasion the Labour party and the Liberal Democrats voted with the Government. Most Bills go through on the nod once they reach the third reading stage but in this case there was obviously a great deal of unease in the Conservative party about the Government's policy on Europe.

19

MASSACRE AT NEWBURY

'*Je ne regrette rien,*' Norman Lamont told voters in Newbury. Was he kidding? With the level of unemployment we are suffering, businesses going bankrupt and him everyone's favourite scapegoat? It has to be one of the most crass and untimely statements made in the recent past by a government minister.

I trust he regretted his words when the Liberal Democrat chants of 'Easy, easy,' filled the dawn air at the racecourse where the count took place. The people of Newbury told the Tories what they thought of them in no uncertain terms. The by-election had to be held because of the tragically sudden death of Judith Chaplin, whom I had known for many years. When I was running the Small Business Association and she was head of the policy unit at the Institute of Directors, we would have lunch at their palatial offices in Pall Mall and I used to feed her anecdotes about small businesses which were being crippled by regulations, most of them emanating from Europe, for her to weave into directors' speeches. She became my line to 10 Downing Street when she went there to work for John Major with whom she had already worked closely at the Treasury.

The Newbury by-election was held on 6 May, the same day as the county council elections, and we were massacred on both counts. In Newbury the Liberal Democrats converted a Conservative majority of 12,367 into a sensational

Lib-Dem gain of 22,055. We also lost control of twenty-four county councils. It's not unusual for the governing party to lose between parliamentary elections but coupled with the abysmal performance in the counties it made depressing reading.

But the news was not all grim. The constituencies with a Euro-rebel Conservative MP did better than average. Sometimes the contrast was spectacular. Having spotted this anomaly I whizzed out a press release to bring it to the attention of the media:

ANTI-MAASTRICHT MPs HAVE BUCKED THE TREND

Examination of the results in the county council elections show a remarkable state of affairs. Well-known Euro-rebel MPs have held on to their county council seats against the national trend. In some areas the results were startling.

In Milton Keynes South West, Barry Legg, one of the Fresh Start group, held two out of three seats, while next door in Milton Keynes North East, Peter Butler, who supported the Government's line, lost.

In Luton North, John Carlisle, a vocal opponent of Europe, held thirteen out of fourteen seats, while in Luton South, Graham Bright, the Prime Minister's well-known PPS, lost out.

But the most sensational result was Teddy Taylor's, in Southend East. He held them all, whereas next door in Castlepoint, which had been Conservative as long as anyone could remember, the pro-Europe member, Robert Spinks, lost the lot.

> Even in Billericay we held three out of four
> seats, one with a hugely increased majority.

The county council elections and Newbury should have sent a strong signal to the Government to reconsider its position urgently. But the Prime Minister announced immediately afterwards that there would be no change in his policies.

As the scale of our losses sank in, one newspaper described us as 'shell-shocked' and that was a good description of how many of us felt. Lifelong Conservative voters in Newbury complained. 'The whole country can't be wrong. They had better get the message and do something about it,' said one.

Another commented, 'In thirteen months John Major has set back the cause of the Tory party more than anyone has done in fifty years.'

But they don't know the man. I wonder if any of us do.

'Nobody knows me,' he told a journalist in an interview. Nor did the Euro-sceptics when they voted for him in preference to the distinctly committed Euro-fan and Foreign Secretary, Douglas Hurd, or the charismatic Michael Heseltine.

John told the party conference in 1991, 'I want the job, I've got it and I'm going to keep it.' Yet the people in the country, first at Newbury then again at Christchurch, as soon as they got the chance sent him a clear message that they don't consider he is doing the job properly.

That's because, in my opinion, John Major has steered Britain into a position where what remains of the power of the Prime Minister is being inexorably drained away to a bunch of foreigners. When this process is complete the job he so dearly wants to hang on to will be more like that of a middle manager, with decisions being made for him by a board of directors in Brussels. Yes, he can try to influence them but, ultimately, those decisions will not be his responsibility.

My message to the Government then was that you can save the situation by giving the electorate the chance to express their views by holding a referendum on the Maastricht treaty. Those election results should have sent a strong signal to the Government to reconsider its position. Instead the Prime Minister dismissed the thrashing we had received by saying complacently that people were determined to give the Government a bloody nose.

When, two months later, he threw down the gauntlet by moving a vote of confidence, we knew we could not, in all conscience, force a general election on either our vulnerable colleagues or the country. We knew the electorate would not be content with a bloody nose. They would have delivered a bloody corpse.

20

GETTING YOUR MOT

The Danish people may have voted No to the Maastricht treaty in June 1992 but their government was determined to overturn their vote. The Danes had expressed their misgivings on a number of issues.

At a meeting of the EC partners held in Edinburgh in December 1992 a deal was stitched up which allowed the Danes to opt out of joint defence policy, a single currency, economic policy obligations and European citizenship. In effect they were not agreeing to give up their sovereignty as our government was on our behalf.

Edinburgh provided a choice example of the way in which deals are made in the EC – not on principle but on expediency. The Spanish Prime Minister, Señor Felipe Gonzales, a friend of Tristan Garel-Jones who was in charge of the negotiations for us and who was up there to advise John Major, had come to Edinburgh with a large financial request in his briefcase. For his own political purposes he wanted to spend £7 billion on a hydrolitic scheme for the north of Spain to install one of the largest irrigation projects in Europe. The Spanish already use more water per head of population than any other country in the Community to grow yet more olives, grapes and other crops to add to the excesses generated by the system of subsidies operated under the Common Agricultural Policy. There was a lot of bitterness, not to say bewilderment, in the country about these mega-expensive follies which we were forced to help finance.

Six months before the Maastricht treaty completed its passage through Parliament, the news leaked out that Tristan Garel-Jones would be giving up his job in the Government as soon as he had completed his task of piloting the Bill through the House. Like Norman Fowler before him, he wanted to spend more time with his family – in the family home in Madrid, where incidentally, John and Norma Major had spent several summer holidays.

During the referendum debate in the Lords, Lord Harris of High Cross said, 'I have a new reason for wanting a referendum, which should cause rejoicing in some quarters. So far the construction of European union has been the handiwork of a narrow political caucus – I would say an exclusive élite – who boast of their linguistic skills and their fastidious nose for fine claret rather than for a pint of good old wallop.'

At about seven thirty one evening as I strolled through an almost deserted members' lobby, when the rest of the House presumably were at dinner, I came across Garel-Jones, who had Walter Sweeney, one of our bravest Euro-sceptics and a new boy, pinned to the base of the statue of Clement Attlee. He appeared to be holding an animated conversation with Walter who stood looking blankly at him, like a naughty schoolboy hauled up before the beak. I walked past and on into the Commons' chamber to listen to a little of the debate. Twenty minutes later, when I came out again, there they were, still at it. I decided to see whether Walter needed help. 'Don't let this man bully you, Walter,' I said, referring to the rough time he had been given by the Whips on the paving debate. 'You're a British patriot but Tristan here is a European. That's something quite different.'

161

'He's trying to give me a hard time, but I think I'm managing all right,' said Walter, in his usual self-deprecating but always polite manner. Garel-Jones, a head shorter than Walter, continued to glare at the knot in his tie.

'Have you had dinner yet, Walter? Would you like to join me? I'm just going to the members' dining room?' I said brightly.

At this, Garel-Jones spun round and looked at me, his face contorted in an evil sort of smile.

'This woman, Walter, is not a Conservative at all. In 1974 she stood against the Conservative candidate in Streatham. She is a Johnny-come-lately. You'll only learn bad habits from her,' he spat out.

This was a reference to my first foray into politics in the second election of 1974 when Edward Heath was prime minister and we were on a three-day week. Ironically, the feeling in the country then mirrors the situation today: people were disillusioned and exasperated with the Tories. Heath didn't seem to be in touch and certainly his policies were pretty unpopular. I had had nothing to do with politics in those days but a group of small business people – there were only half a dozen of us – decided we would put up our own candidate because we despaired at the official Conservative policies – a bit like now! We drew lots for which of us should stand as an Independent candidate and I got the short straw. I was much more of a shrinking violet then and because I was worried that the neighbours would think I was barmy I stood in my maiden name, Moore, so that when I pushed the literature through their door they wouldn't realize it was me.

I paid my deposit in gold Krugerrands as a protest, to demonstrate how our paper money was becoming worthless

– we had 20 per cent inflation – and there was a terrific to-do when we presented ourselves at Brixton Town Hall. All the national newspapers reported the story, but it was the only press coverage I managed to get during the run-up to the election.

My supporters and I succeeded in making three separate deliveries to each of 36,000 homes, which just shows that you can run a campaign with a very small group of people. It was wonderful fun although we only got 300 votes at the end of it. Once, I was going down the high street in a van with my loudspeaker and stopped opposite the Tories' van – we were bonnet to bonnet – and Bill Shelton shouted at me through his loudhailer, 'Why are you doing this to me?'

'Because the Conservatives are not doing it for me,' I retorted through my loudhailer. It was hilarious, the two of us shouting at each other like that in the street. Afterwards, he invited Jim and me to the Pugin Room in the Commons for a cup of tea and tried to persuade us to join the Conservative party. Later he master-minded Margaret's campaign for the leadership and after she became leader I joined and threw myself into becoming an active member.

'Well, that's not so disreputable as selling your country to the Europeans,' I answered Garel-Jones, smiling sweetly. 'And I believe even the great Winston Churchill changed his political position more than once.'

Poor Walter looked bemused. A natural gentleman, he didn't quite know what to do to defuse this acrimonious conversation. 'Why don't you go off to the tea room while Tristan and I sort out Europe?' I said, to give him the opportunity to escape.

'Why don't you piss off?' said Garel-Jones.

This is pretty mild stuff by his standards. While serving

in the Whips' office he acquired a reputation for terrorizing with his tongue even senior members of the party who appeared to be straying from the party line. Sir George Gardiner, who did not suffer as much bullying from the Whips as some of us did, told me, 'The only foul language I have heard was from Tristan Garel-Jones in the taxi queue, in which the Maastricht rebels were described in every other sentence as either "traitors" or "wankers".' Tristan was a powerful figure in the party when he was in the Whips' office. Now he was the Prime Minister's right-hand man.

The Danish refusal to ratify the treaty except on their own terms gave Gonzales the opportunity he needed. He simply refused to agree to the Danish opt-outs unless and until he was given a promise of £7 billion to come from the new Cohesion Fund, to be created under Maastricht. And he got his way. So did the Danes. Given that they had effectively neutralized the Maastricht treaty as far as they were concerned, it seemed to me a great pity that the British Government didn't insist on the same opt-outs. It would have put a lot of people's minds at rest within Euro-rebel circles.

And now once again the Prime Minister was at the dispatch box telling us what a wonderful deal he had fixed up for everyone at Edinburgh. The Danish No campaigners, all volunteers, who had exhausted their funds and the enthusiasm of many of their workers, had to gear up again to re-fight their original battle. With all the resources of the Danish Government at their disposal the Yes campaigners had the advantage. There was a great deal of to-ing and fro-ing between Denmark and Britain: the Danes were buoyed up by the campaign we were mounting here; we were impressed by their courage and tenacity. Bill Cash and others raised funds in the UK to help them, and a number of MPs, including some from the Labour party, kept up a stream of visits to do what they could but to no avail. This time, the Danes, no doubt bored and irritated by the whole procedure, voted Yes.

It was a sad vote for British Euro-sceptics and especially for those who were now organizing two different polls. One, launched by Margaret Thatcher, David Alton and Bryan Gould, invited people to telephone their votes for or against holding a referendum. The other, organized by Bill Cash, backed by Sir James Goldsmith and launched by Russell Lewis and Sir Martin Garrod, took the form of a petition for which we hoped to get at least a million signatures. In the event there were 250,000. Neither was as successful as had been hoped but both revealed a strong feeling in the country that citizens should be given a say in this momentous decision.

21

THE NIGHT OF
THE SHORT
KNIVES

When the committee stage was over, the Prime Minister seized the opportunity to reshuffle his Cabinet. Norman Lamont was the man who was going to carry the can for Britain being bounced out of the ERM and Garel-Jones was getting out. But there was another old score to settle.

It was two in the afternoon and the telephone rang on Edward Leigh's desk in his office at the Department of Trade and Industry where he was a junior minister.

'The Prime Minister would like to see you. Could you come over straight away?'

Edward replaced the phone. Unusual. Must be something serious. Perhaps the chop? Of the dozen or more people in the Government who were anti-Maastricht he was the most indiscreet.

'I'm Edward Leigh, and I've got an appointment with the Prime Minister,' he told the policeman at the new wrought-iron security gates which now guard the entrance to Downing Street.

The policeman consulted his list. 'Yes, sir, come through.'

A handful of tourists looked on with mild curiosity.

Anyone passing through this barricade must be someone important.

They're hardly likely to know who I am, Edward thought, remembering a conversation he had had a couple of weeks before with a taxi driver taking him home across the river Humber to his Lincolnshire constituency.

'Some kind of politician are you?'

'Yes.'

'What's your name?'

'Edward Leigh.'

'Never heard of you!'

Edward smiled.

It was ten past two and the policeman outside the door of 10 Downing Street nodded.

'Good afternoon, sir.'

'Edward Leigh.'

'Yes, sir, you're expected.'

Before the policeman could knock, the door of No. 10 opened. They had already been alerted that Edward was on his way. A member of staff was waiting inside the entrance hall. 'Please follow me. We're going to the Cabinet Room.'

Edward felt a short burst of panic as he entered the long Cabinet Room where, two and a half years earlier, he had waited at six o'clock in the morning in a vain attempt to persuade Margaret Thatcher to fight the second ballot for the leadership.

The Prime Minister was seated half-way down the long table. Edward walked along and sat opposite in the seat usually reserved for the Chancellor.

John Major looked up. 'Don't sit there, Edward. Come

and sit beside me,' and he patted the chair. 'It's always a painful business reconstructing the Government . . .'

Edward knew then that this was it. He was determined not to show any emotion. The fate of a junior minister is only important to himself and his family. He expected a few emollient words and that would be that.

'You're a man of conviction. I would admire you less if you weren't. You can't change. There is no question of your competence. Quite the contrary. But in Westminster's hot-house your criticism of policies and personalities in the Government is well known. In difficult times it is better to have a united team.'

It was two fifteen. Edward was one of the founder members of the No Turning Back group. As he walked back to his office in Victoria Street he reflected that others in the group were still apparently safe inside the Cabinet. But for how long? Would they, too, be purged for a lack of political correctness?

They were just as much out of sympathy with Maastricht. And not just Maastricht. People who believe in free trade, low taxes, minimum regulations and customer choice could hardly support the European Community as it has turned out.

It was a pointer to the Prime Minister's priorities that he had been prepared to tolerate the shenanigans of David Mellor and Michael Mates but not opposition to his European policies from a junior member of the Government.

As Edward reached the door at Downing Street it was hurriedly flung open. Daylight flooded in. A group of photographers was in the street snapping the winners and losers. Like those silly barometers, Lamont went in smiling and came out scowling. Kenneth Clarke arrived scowling and came out smiling. Well, he would, wouldn't he? His credentials on European union were much more to the Prime

Minister's taste. Strangely enough, Edward felt happy. He certainly did not feel bitter about what John Major had just done to him. Of course, he reflected, he is entitled to sack people he doesn't want on his team.

Edward told us later he had been thinking of resigning over Maastricht for months. He had talked the matter over with his friends in the No Turning Back group, including Portillo, Lilley and Redwood who had tried to persuade him not to.

'What will it achieve?' they asked him. 'Nothing. Keep fighting from within. Don't resign. It would look temperamental. Pointless.'

But Edward, an honourable person, said he felt increasingly uncomfortable because through all these months he had voted for a treaty which he knew was bad for the country. Before the third reading he asked the Whips if he could be sent somewhere and miss the vote.

No chance, they told him.

Now he had to live with the knowledge that he had betrayed his own conscience and put the interests of the Government before those of the country, which is exactly what MPs in the 1930s had lived to regret doing over Chamberlain's appeasement policy.

Edward had tried to work within the government. At one stage he went, as a spokesman for fourteen junior ministers, directly to the Prime Minister expressing their worries over the threat posed by the European Court which could override decisions of our own Parliament.

After the first Danish referendum he wrote to the Prime Minister begging for a free vote in the House of Commons to reunite the party. The Prime Minister dismissed the idea, just as Margaret Thatcher had dismissed criticism of her poll tax. Looking back, he mused, it was surprising that the Prime Minister hadn't got rid of him earlier.

Edward's mind came back to the Lincolnshire taxi driver. As he drove off he had shouted, 'I'll never bother to vote again. You're all the bloody same. You don't believe in anything.'

Norman Lamont was more bitter about getting the push than Edward. He had piloted the Prime Minister's policy on the ERM, taken the flak, and now that the economy was showing some signs of recovery, someone else was going to get the glory.

A fall from high office is never comfortable and Norman looked less than pleased when he emerged from No. 10. At that level you don't just lose your position, the whole family is affected. There's the move from the flat at 11 Downing Street, the loss of the weekend place in the country where flunkeys cater to your every need, the entertaining, the chauffeur-driven car, the deferential attitude of everyone from the lady who pushes the tea trolley round the Treasury to the Lord Mayor of London or the President of the CBI. And, of course, there is a drop in salary. On the other hand you don't have to lie through your teeth, which must be something of a consolation for a decent man like Norman.

Everyone, but everyone, wants to be on good terms with the Chancellor. But a minister relegated to the back benches is pretty far down the pecking order. From now on an occasional newspaper correspondent in search of a good story or a City banker sniffing out inside information may treat you to lunch at the Savoy but that's about it. All he can look forward to is writing his memoirs unless, of course, he is lucky enough to be offered a directorship of a City bank which is what has happened to Norman. For a junior minister like Edward, telling your side of the story to the *Spectator* offers some consolation.

Neil Hamilton, another minister at the Department of Trade and Industry, a close friend of Edward's, received a telephone call.

'Hello, Neil, it's Tristan,' the smooth dark one said. 'I think you should have a word with your friend Edward Leigh. If he doesn't keep his mouth shut he'll be dead meat.'

'Really?' said Neil. 'How are you going to bring that about?'

'I know plenty of people at the top end of his constituency association. I can easily get some speaking engagements up there and dish the dirt on him. It won't take much to get him removed.'

Neil paused. He was not the man to be intimidated by Garel-Jones. 'If you feel like that, why don't you go and stand against him at the election?'

'That might not be a bad idea. I've got boundary changes in my area and I might just be looking for another seat.'

'Well, best of luck.'

The subject of Edward came up at our regular Fresh Start meeting.

'I have had a proposal that Edward Leigh should be admitted to this group,' said Michael, opening the meeting. 'I want to get the feeling of colleagues on this.'

'Yes. I think we should. It's a gesture to a colleague who has paid the price for his prinicples,' said Trevor Skeet.

'I strongly disagree. All of us round this table have fought this thing through without support from the people inside the Government. If they'd had the courage to vote with us on the paving debate we could have killed it then and there,' said someone else.

'I'm very much opposed,' said Ann Winterton. 'We have come through this together and forged a bond of trust between us. We come from all sides of the party – we wouldn't normally be found in the same boat.'

'I agree with Ann. We don't want to be seen to be picking people up just because they have been jettisoned by someone else. I think it's probably too soon,' said Michael. 'But I'll have a word with Edward and tell him there are no hard feelings. Just that it would be better to let a little water run under the bridge.'

And he added, 'Off the record, I know that Edward has been working very hard within the Government. He told me he went to the Prime Minister to ask for a free vote in the Commons after Black Wednesday.'

'White Wednesday,' Tony Marlow corrected him.

'You're right, Tony. It's the best thing that has happened to the economy for a very long time. I believe Edward also wanted to be somewhere else when it came to the vote on the third reading.'

'All he had to do was abstain. All they could have done was sack him. And they've done that anyway. It's better to be sacked for your principles than pushed out,' said another colleague.

'Has anyone been approached by Norman Lamont yet?' Nick Budgen asked.

'Not yet. But it could happen,' said Michael, to laughter.

22

ACTION
STATIONS

I t was three months to the day since the committee stage
finished and two months since the reshuffle. The Fresh
Start group continued its regular meetings and at the
first one that week, Monday 19 July, Michael Spicer reported
an approach he had had from the Government.

'Richard Ryder has just contacted me with an eleventh-
hour offer. The Government will commit itself to no re-entry
to the ERM in the lifetime of this Parliament, a specific
commitment they have not made before, if we promise not
to vote for further obstructions to the Bill on Thursday.
What are your views?' he asked us.

This was a sensation and we had a lengthy discussion.
Everyone had their say but the majority view was that it was
too late and not worth very much because the country
probably wouldn't re-enter the ERM anyway.

'OK. If that's your verdict I shall tell Richard Ryder we
reject the Government's offer.'

During the committee stage, to diffuse the possibility of
losing a vote, the Government had agreed that after the Bill
was safely through the House of Commons, there would be
a special vote on the opt-out part of the Maastricht treaty
which dealt with working conditions, the so-called social
chapter. The Government reasoned that it hardly mattered
whether Parliament voted for or against it at that stage. But
others thought differently.

The Labour party wanted the social chapter back in the treaty. We reasoned that, if we voted with them, the Government would have to jettison the whole Bill. It had pledged that it would not ratify the treaty if the social chapter were in.

On the evening before the all-or-nothing debate, the group met in our bunker.

'This is going to be the big one,' I said to Michael Lord as we walked down the back stairs.

'It means we're going to have to vote with the Labour party for the social chapter. I'm not sure the public will understand why we're doing it,' said Michael, with a shake of his head. 'The media will try to misrepresent our actions. The constituency associations may not understand.'

'They will if you make it clear to them. We're not voting to defeat the Government, but to defeat the Maastricht treaty,' I said with new emphasis. 'What will happen if the Government does lose the vote?'

'If we win, we risk the Prime Minister resigning,' said Michael.

'Not again! He threatened to do that during the paving debate. He can't keep pulling that trick.'

'What they're more likely to do is call for a vote of confidence in the Government. And we will all be able to vote for that. After all, by then we will have achieved our objective of dumping this Bill.'

'It might not be as simple as that. I think they will tie the vote of confidence to government policy, something like a vote of confidence in the ratification of the treaty. That is going to make it a lot more difficult.'

'When will they call the vote? Monday?'

'I doubt it. They'll do it on Friday morning. They'll want

to get it out of the way to prevent speculation in the press over the weekend.'

'I'll see what I can find out,' said Michael.

A handful of colleagues was already seated round the long table, chatting.

'Where should I sit?' I said.

'Up here. This is the whip's end.' Michael sat in his usual seat at the head of the table.

'That's Bill's seat. He always sits on your right hand,' I quipped.

'No. James Cran usually sits here.' I hadn't noticed because he doesn't say much; Bill usually does all the talking. It was true that James Cran and Christopher Gill said little at these meetings: whips are there to watch and listen. But it was difficult to turn Bill Cash off.

The banter was light-hearted and friendly. By now, we all knew each other well. Amazingly, we all seemed to get on. As I looked round the table I realized that Ann and I were now 'one of the chaps'. Everyone was still charming and complimentary to me as a woman but when I put my point of view they listened and took me seriously. At least, I think they did!

Now the room was fairly full. Twenty-six people present. A good turn-out.

'I have no need to tell you how important it is for us to hold on to our position tomorrow. The pressure is on again from constituency officers, leaned on by Central Office, and I know some colleagues are unhappy at the prospect of voting for the social chapter to go back in,' said Michael, opening the meeting.

'There is no way I can vote for this social chapter,' said Rupert Allason. I was surprised he was there: I couldn't remember seeing him with us before. He wasn't even on my mailing list of Fresh Start members; someone else must have told him about the meeting.

'Half my constituents work in the fishing industry and they've already had a terrible time from the European legislation. And the other half earn their living from the tourist trade. They rely on seasonal and part-time labour. The conditions of employment in the social chapter would cripple them. They're already having a bad enough time because of the recession. There is no way I could vote for it,' he said firmly.

'Don't they understand that if we ditch the treaty we'll ditch the social chapter with it?' asked Richard Shepherd, sitting opposite him across the table.

'You understand that and so do I. But I don't think the people in my constituency will. This will be portrayed as me supporting regulations that will kill the industry. Much as I hate this treaty, I can't vote for that.'

'But you could abstain. Surely you could explain that to your constituents?' said Michael Spicer. 'We understand the predicament you're in, but this is our last chance to get rid of the whole thing.'

A number of people supported Rupert's position; there was obviously considerable unease.

'I think some of our colleagues will use the argument that voting with the socialists is unacceptable at any price and make it an excuse to vote with the Government,' said Ann Winterton. 'Even people we have been able to rely upon in the past. Of course, a lot of those who've abstained lately will probably go through the government lobby, too,' she added.

'I do advise you to go away and read the Prime Minister's

words. He has assured us that he will not accept the treaty with the social chapter,' said Sir Trevor Skeet, a New Zealander. Now in his seventies he is as fit and sprightly as anyone round the table and was one of our stalwarts throughout.

In the early days, when Michael Spicer was recruiting people to our group, he met Trevor in the tea room. 'We're forming a group to oppose this wretched treaty, Trevor. What about joining?'

'I'll go away and read the treaty and then I'll let you know,' said Trevor briskly. True to his word, he did.

'You have my full support. Dreadful business. Awful treaty. Nothing left of parliamentary democracy if we adopt it. Do everything I can to defeat the Bill. Count me in.' From then on, he never wavered.

'I believe invitations have been flying around to meet the Prime Minister. Has anyone here been?' asked Michael.

People stirred. 'I was invited to see the Prime Minister. I had thirty minutes with him in a private conversation and I cannot reveal what was said,' said Sir Peter Tapsell. 'But I can say that I assured the Prime Minister that I saw this as a major constitutional issue and advised him to change his mind. I am sure he respects my position.'

'I received the invitation, too,' said John Wilkinson, looking down at the table. 'Unfortunately, I was too busy so I had to turn the invitation down.' We laughed again. John Wilkinson was one of the most reliable of our group: a fierce patriot, he also saw the treaty as a threat to our sovereignty.

'I had the same offer,' said Nicholas Winterton. 'And I know this group would not expect me to reveal the contents of the discussion. But I can say what I told the Prime Minister: if he could assure me that we will never go back into the Exchange Rate Mechanism I will reconsider my position.'

'Well, that shouldn't be difficult, and did he give you that assurance?' asked Iain Duncan-Smith. 'Because he didn't give it to me.'

'Some hope,' said Richard Shepherd.

'Can't you tell us what the Prime Minister said?' asked Michael. 'After all, if he gave the assurance, it might help our discussion.'

Nicholas, never reluctant to give his views, remained silent. I thought it odd. Nicholas was famous for his run-ins with the Government; he was far from being a soft target. As chairman of a select committee on the health service he had been vocal in his criticism of government moves to create trusts out of public hospitals and the Government had punished him by ousting him from the chairmanship with the co-operation of Sir Marcus Fox.

As I looked round the table it was interesting to speculate why certain people had been invited to see the Prime Minister. I can't imagine anyone thinking John Wilkinson could be turned. Sir Peter Tapsell was different: he came from the left of the party so perhaps they thought for that reason he could be persuaded. Nicholas Winterton? Why should the Whips think it worthwhile subjecting him, of all people, to the Prime Minister's undoubted charm unless they had something particular to offer him?

'I will abstain,' said Bernard Jenkin. He had abstained most of the time. Other freshmen, like his friend John Whittingdale, had long since given up coming to our meetings and now voted with the Government all the time.

'What are the Ulster Unionists doing? I believe they're

being heavily leaned on. Rumour has it they've been offered something. Do you know anything about it, Roger?' asked Michael.

Roger Knapman was our liaison with the Unionists. Back in 1991, when he was PPS to Archie Hamilton in the Defence Ministry, Roger had resigned over Maastricht. 'Ian Paisley and Peter Robinson are solid, but they're not too sure about James Molyneaux's group.'

The Ulster Unionists were divided into the Paisleyites, who sat on the Conservative benches, and James Molyneaux's supporters, who sat with Labour in protest at the Anglo-Irish Agreement.

'It's hard to believe the Government will give them what *they* really want – an end to the Anglo-Irish Agreement. Having come this far, I'd be surprised if James Molyneaux could be bought off,' said Toby Jessel.

'I think the Government is worried enough perhaps to make us some concessions. Would you like me to try and meet with Richard Ryder to see whether we can do any deals?' asked Michael.

'There is only one deal worth doing, and that is the promise of a referendum,' said Teddy Taylor. 'And they're hardly likely to give us that.'

'If they're that worried about us you might be able to squeeze some concessions out of them. Maybe a promise, as Nick says, to abandon the ERM for good.'

'That would knock the guts out of the treaty. Without monetary union there is really nothing left. Unless there is to be a single currency and a central bank, the Germans won't be able to exercise their control over the Community,' said Peter Tapsell.

'Well, I can try. I agree the Government is extremely nervous – much more nervous than they were in the paving debate. This time they believe we can win.'

As the meeting broke up Christopher Gill came across to me. 'We'll need someone to see which of our colleagues goes through each lobby at the vote,' he said to me. 'Will you cover the No lobby and I'll do the Ayes?' he asked.

'Of course. Although it will hardly matter by then who went through.'

'True, but it will be nice to know. We can't guarantee there won't be another vote early next week. If the Government loses they're bound to force another vote. A straight vote of confidence in the Government would be easy, but they may have something else up their sleeves.'

Later that evening, Michael Spicer was eating dinner in the strangers' cafeteria in the basement, the House of Commons equivalent of the works canteen. After eight o'clock, we joked, even the gravy refused to move about.

'May we join you?' Michael, who was thumbing through the *Evening Standard*, looked up. Two cabinet ministers, Michael Howard and Peter Lilley, trays in hand, stood over him. He was more than a little surprised.

'Do, please. It's very nice to see you down here at the cheaper end of the market.' They laughed. They were old friends; they had all served in the Government together and they shared the same political position to the right of the party.

'I'm very flattered to get two cabinet ministers. Most people have to make do with their Whip. On second thoughts, of course, some people have been asked to see the Prime Minister.'

'We cannot compete with that,' said Peter Lilley.

180

'You don't have to,' said Michael, 'he hasn't asked to see me. I suppose you've come down here to lean on me a little. I hope I won't spoil your dinner if I say that you're not going to change my mind.'

'But we have to go through the motions,' said Michael Howard.

'Just so long as you don't spoil my appetite.'

The tiny strangers' dining room was crowded, the tables packed together. Next to them John Carlisle and Michael Lord of our group listened.

'Of course, I could turn this request round and try to persuade you to vote with us tomorrow,' said Michael.

'Not a chance,' said Michael Howard.

All round the dining room, heads were turning in their direction; everyone knew what this not-so-casual encounter was about and was curious to hear what was being said.

The House was agog with anticipation about to-morrow's debate in which the Government was seriously in danger of getting another bloody nose only two months after the Newbury by-election.

23

PANTO
TIME

Momentous debates in the House of Commons are like pantomimes. There are the two principal boys with a chorus of courtiers in attendance. There are the villains of the piece who come in from stage right and cause mayhem.

Presumably our principal boy would class me as one of them although I, of course, see my role as the Good Fairy fighting to save us from the evil kingdom. There is the pantomime dame who tonight would tickle our ribs until we were crying with laughter. There are odd sketches which seem to have nothing to do with the main plot. And there is the audience, thoroughly enjoying themselves, hissing and booing to their hearts' content.

Like all the best pantomimes, the tale of Maastricht is simple but it has been transformed into a cunningly devious plot, the better to bamboozle the paying public who wouldn't pay two pence for it if they could see what a shabby piece of nonsense it really is.

Ever since he returned from negotiating the Maastricht treaty in November 1991, the Prime Minister had sought to reassure the House not so much about the treaty's virtues but about the opt-outs. No social chapter and no headlong rush into monetary union. Yippee. That's all right, then.

To those of us who oppose the treaty, it seems incredible

that its main appeal to the Prime Minister appeared to be the bits he managed to leave out. Not that we believed this would make a blind bit of difference.

I made a point of this at Question Time. I put it to him: 'Does my Right Honourable Friend agree that the social chapter issue is a red herring? And that if we sign up to Maastricht the European Court will have the power to impose the conditions upon us whether we vote for them or not? And, therefore, those people who do not want the social chapter inflicted on us should vote tonight to defeat ratification?'

As always Prince Charming was affable and friendly in his reply. 'This is one of those rare occasions when I am unable to share the view of my Honourable Friend. I believe she is entirely wrong and I hope she will reconsider her position before ten o'clock.'

The House erupted noisily.

There were shouts of 'Hear, hear!'

'Change your mind, Teresa.'

'Give in.'

'Make her a Dame,' shouted someone on the Labour benches.

'Order! Order!' bellowed Betty Boothroyd. 'You can save all that for later.'

The House, in anticipation of the fireworks to come, was already in a state of high excitement. This was the debate the Labour party had been waiting for, we had been working for and the Tories dreaded, a gladiatorial contest where the champions on each side, John Major and John Smith, would be defending those parts of the treaty in which they took most pride. The Government was on a knife edge: the tension showed in the faces of the Conservative front bench.

The Labour party looked more relaxed. Hold on to your seats, I thought, we're in for a bumpy ride.

A few days before, Lord Rees-Mogg, a former editor of *The Times* and a pillar of the Establishment, announced he was taking the Government to court on certain aspects of the treaty. Strongly opposed to Maastricht, he hoped to persuade the High Court to rule that the Government's handling of the ratification was unconstitutional. His financial backer was multi-millionaire Sir James Goldsmith. Would Lord Rees-Mogg's action prevent the House from discussing the treaty while the courts were considering it?

Betty Boothroyd dealt with this point first. 'I have been made aware of an interest in the possible application of the House's *sub judice* rules to today's debate. I wish to announce at the outset that I have decided not to apply these *sub judice* rules today.' That settled that.

The Prime Minister rose. People were standing at the bar, which is actually just a line painted on the floor. In the old days there was a wooden bar across and anyone behind it was not technically in the chamber and could not contribute to a debate from that position. Some MPs had to sit in the aisles. Norma and James Major were watching anxiously from the galleries as John fought for his political life.

Not long into the Prime Minister's speech Michael Lord, a long-standing member of the Fresh Start group, rose to intervene. 'Will the Prime Minister give way?' he cried. By getting there early, I had managed to reserve a grandstand view two rows behind the PM. Michael was two rows behind me. I noticed Major bowed his head as if concentrating, or maybe he had his ear to the microphone to make sure he didn't miss a word.

Every pantomime has its well-rehearsed sub-plots and this is one which was going to shake some of us rigid.

'My Right Honourable Friend knows that for many years I have opposed the social chapter because of the effect it would have on companies such as ICI in Stowmarket in my constituency,' Michael said, achieving the time-honoured wheeze of getting your voters a mention. 'I urge the Prime Minister to continue to oppose the social chapter as strongly as he can. I will be voting against the social chapter and in support of the Government in the lobby tonight.'

I spun round. I could hardly believe my ears. This was an abdication worthy of a Soviet show trial. There was uproar. I caught the eye of Sir Peter Tapsell sitting in the row immediately behind me to my right. 'I can't believe it,' I said to him above the noise. 'Michael has been one of us all along.'

Peter's face showed no response, but he raised his shoulders in a gesture of dismissal. Giles Radice, the Labour member for Durham North and a dedicated Euro-fanatic, shouted something. It sounded like 'Hear, hear!'

The Prime Minister's reply to Michael made it perfectly obvious that the whole incident had been stage-managed. Michael had not only decided to desert our cause at the eleventh hour, he had agreed to eat humble pie publicly. The derision on the Labour benches, the shouts of support from the Euro-fan Tories continued for several minutes. Only Euro-rebels on both sides of the House remained silent.

The Prime Minister continued with his speech, but not for long. John Carlisle, the member for Luton North and another of our stalwarts, was next to rise. 'Will the Prime Minister give way?' he asked.

185

Again, as if prearranged, which it obviously was, the Prime Minister sat down.

'I am grateful to my Right Honourable Friend for giving way,' John began. I turned again to look at my fellow conspirator. Was this another traitor? Peter stared stonily ahead. John was sitting immediately behind him. 'Perhaps you would like to know the facts which have made me change my mind and support the Government tonight?'

His words seemed to be directed as much to his erstwhile colleagues in the Fresh Start group as to the House.

'Any more turncoats?' yelled someone from the Labour benches.

'Give 'im a job, John.'

The Prime Minister rose again, but before he could speak, Peter stood up. 'Will my Right Honourable Friend give way?' he boomed.

'Not another one!' shouted someone from the Labour benches.

'Hear, hear! Yes, please,' shouted people on the Tory benches.

Betty stood up. 'Order!' she cried. 'The House wants to hear what the Prime Minister says. We are wasting time.'

I knew Peter would throw a brickbat and I waited, tense, for the thud. The Prime Minister turned, looked at Peter, then gestured and sat down again.

Peter waited until the noise died away. 'May I congratulate the Prime Minister on his latest converts?' he said contemptuously.

The mood of the House changed in a matter of seconds. This was high drama. I turned round. 'Well said,' I called out.

186

The Prime Minister was on his feet again, delivering an off-the-cuff response which was clearly well prepared.

'I'm always delighted to accept a sinner returning home. I am delighted to see my Honourable Friends back supporting the Government.' Then he turned to concentrate on the group he wanted us all to boo most loudly that evening, to label the most despised villains of the piece: the Liberal Democrat party.

'As for them, I find their position incomprehensible. Given their previous statements, it is frankly contemptible.' This was a reference to the fact that the Liberal Democrats, who had supported the Government all through these many months, were about to go into the lobby with Labour in support of the social chapter. The Liberal Democrats also wanted the Maastricht treaty warts and all.

His remarks provoked Paddy Ashdown to his feet, something which was guaranteed to be greeted with catcalls. Everyone knocks Paddy, calling him Action Man, Captain Mainwaring or the Boy from Bosnia. Yet despite the barracking he invariably receives, he is one of the best performers.

'It is true my party has reservations about the social chapter, but we believe it is in the country's interests to be inside the treaty changing them, not outside complaining about them.'

What irony! That Paddy should make this remark at this stage when, less than twenty-four hours later, the Prime Minister was to make a similar remark referring to the 'Bastards' in his Cabinet. Although Major was too coy to quote Lyndon Johnson in full – 'I'd rather have my enemies inside the tent pissing out, than outside pissing in' – everyone knows that this is what he was really saying when he talked about the Bastards.

The PM bobbed up again. 'I recall going fishing many years ago when somebody caught an eel. "My," they said. "Look how it wriggles." Wriggle though the Right Honourable Gentleman may [there he goes with his wriggle word, again], I will quote what he has said in the past. "I am not going to vote for Labour for one night of fun at the Government's expense and ask the British people to pay in more lost jobs." Does the Right Honourable Gentleman still believe that or not?'

I began to edge forward waiting for an opportunity to join in the debate. I could feel my heart beginning to pound. I knew the Prime Minister would give way to me if I got to my feet, expecting another convert.

Just then Simon Burns jumped up. 'Does my Right Honourable Friend agree that eels are excessively slippery?' The House erupted. The Prime Minister loved it, he could talk about wriggling till the cows came home.

'This is becoming more fun than I had imagined.'

As he spoke I got to my feet and gestured towards him. 'Teresa, Teresa.' The chant broke out on the Tory benches. Hands were stretched towards me. 'Come on, Teresa, it's your turn to rejoin the Government.' The noise was so loud it was impossible for me to be heard. I became calmer and waited until they went quiet.

'She's turning, she's turning,' yelled people all around me.

I put both hands on my hips in a defiant gesture and turned to the right then to the left, looking along the benches, savouring the moment. Slowly I shook my head.

'The lady's not for turning,' yelled Dennis Skinner from the front bench opposite. Uproar broke out again and Betty was on her feet yelling, but no one took any notice. The Prime Minister turned round and pulled a face.

'Does the Prime Minister agree with me that whether or not we adopt the social chapter, this country's experience with the European Community has taught us that it has many ways of destroying jobs? The fishing industry is practically on its knees. The meat-processing industry is the latest to be decimated by European regulations. During all the years I have run a small business, European regulations have consistently destroyed jobs in this country. The idea that we will be able to control the imposition of regulations on employers in this country is pie in the sky. The triumph of hope over experience.' I ended to a roar of approval and sat down.

Peter Tapsell leaned over and patted me on the shoulder. 'Well done,' he said.

I turned to him. 'Well, at least I won't get a white feather in the post tomorrow morning, unlike the people sitting behind you.' I nodded in the direction of Michael Lord and John Carlisle. Somehow I felt my intervention had purged their treachery and saved the reputation of the Fresh Start group. I felt calm again, having restored our image.

'In that case my Honourable Friend should be in the lobby against the social chapter this evening,' Major replied. 'As a small businesswoman she will know that sixty per cent of our exports go to the European Community and that a massive amount of inward investment comes to every part of this country because of our membership.'

Yes, and I had enough experience to know that having 60 per cent of all your customers in one market is dangerous when that market is going into deep recession. Europe is only 10 per cent of the world's markets and less than 10 per cent of the world's population. Britain's wealth and prosperity has been built up on free trade with the whole world, with countries outside Europe. They are our natural customers and speak our business language. Yet we make it more and more difficult for them to sell us their basic products in an effort to protect the farmers in Europe. We are like Red Indians living inside a stockade of tariffs, hoping to be able to survive while keeping out the goods from the rest of the world. It is alien to the history of Britain as a trading nation. Already we have a massive trade deficit with the European Community yet we are locked into this ludicrous obsession of doing business mainly with it.

I wish with all my heart we could be an offshore island like Hong Kong, a free trade area with the minimum of government intervention and the maximum of business activity. That's what we need to get our economy going again.

My attention was drawn back to the debate when Nicholas Winterton's name was called. I turned. Surely Nick was not going to join the deserters?

'My Right Honourable Friend will know of my strong opposition to and reservations about the Maastricht treaty. I have been greatly encouraged by what he has said about how he envisages Europe's future and the influence he can bring to bear from within. Will the Prime Minister help me by assuring the House that this country will not move towards a single currency and return to the Exchange Rate Mechanism as long as he is in power? Will he assure us that we in this country, who are proud of our sovereignty, integrity and place in the world, will be able to continue to have control over our foreign and security policies?'

What was Nicholas up to? This is the point he had told us yesterday evening he raised with the Prime Minister. Was this part of a strategy planned between them on that occasion? Fresh Start members would appreciate the nuances of what was going on – but would everyone else?

'I have repeatedly said to the House I do not envisage we will be able to move towards a single currency in anything remotely like the timescale previously set out,' said the Prime Minister. 'There is no prospect of our returning to the Exchange Rate Mechanism in the near future as the conditions are simply not right. I do not envisage they will be right for a considerable period of time.'

As usual, the Prime Minister was prevaricating. Surely Nicholas would recognize that? This reply was no different from the devious answer which he always gave when questioned on this subject. Wriggle, wriggle, wriggle.

I turned once more, my face asking Peter Tapsell a silent question. Was Nicholas about to turn? Peter sat stoical, his arms folded across his chest. If he had any views he was keeping them to himself.

But turn Nicholas did. Later that evening he was dragged from the chamber to talk to three Cabinet ministers. Whatever they told him it was enough. He voted with the Government.

The debate raged on. The House was very noisy as other ministers, including Tristan Garel-Jones, rose to interrupt John Smith. On the back benches members were beginning to be irritated by all the quoting from international agencies in support of their side of the argument. It is a tired old ploy and one that is wheeled out far too often.

John Smith managed to raise a titter with his knowledge of comic strip heroes: 'Like Clark Kent, as soon as the Prime

Minister leaves our shores behind, he is transformed into a diplomatic mega-star. There he is, his Superman shirt tucked neatly into his underpants, shaping the very destiny of Europe, clutching his Maastricht opt-out as his colleagues gently take him to the door marked *Sortie*. What the Prime Minister does not understand . . .'

By this stage the Labour benches were rolling about the aisles at the wit and wisdom of their leader. Even some of the Conservatives were smiling. The Speaker was on her feet valiantly trying to regain order by shouting over the noise.

At this point Dame Elaine Kellett-Bowman, the Conservative member for Lancaster, whose voice sounds like a tape that has been put on fast-forward, rose to defend our hero. 'Does the Right Honourable and Learned Gentleman recall what was said in the French press when he returned from his negotiations?' At this point Dame Elaine looked downwards at a newspaper cutting and began to read: 'Holding his own . . .' Before she could go on the House erupted, clutching its collective sides. Everyone, including the people in the galleries above, was rocking with mirth.

Dame Elaine stood there, innocently waiting for the laughter to die down. Her face was expressionless – perhaps she had no idea what they all thought was so funny. Betty Boothroyd, who was having as much trouble containing herself as anyone else, stood up to cry her familiar, 'Order! Order!' Slowly and deliberately, emphasizing every word, she repeated, 'This House must come to order!'

It took a few more minutes for the merriment to die down. Dame Elaine was ready to continue reading the quotation from her newspaper cutting. '. . . holding his own against his eleven partners.' The House collapsed in a hysterical heap. 'The Prime Minister can show he has fought a tenacious battle and resisted the interference of socialists, technocrats and demonstrated his devotion to economic liberalism.' Bemused, she raised her eyes from the paper and gestured with it towards the Opposition. 'That was said in *La Libération*,' she announced triumphantly and, with a gesture of defiance, she resumed her seat.

(Dame Elaine is not the only MP who is unconsciously funny. Geoffrey Dickens is another. He is a serious campaigner on the subject of child abuse but sometimes, when he gets on one of his hobby horses, he gets tongue-tied. He was once going on about 'perverts' and Aids and said, 'I'm sick and tired of these homosexuals thrusting their opinions down my throat.')

John Smith, wiping the tears from his eyes, resumed his place at the dispatch box. 'I want to quote from an interesting article in *The Times* in which the author wrote, "We paid a heavy price when others designed the Common Agricultural Policy. It would be unforgivable to repeat that mistake in industrial and financial policies. The same arguments apply to the social chapter. The issue is whether new policies come here by the back door, following mergers and takeovers, or whether the Government battles to get the original proposals brought more into line with British practices. I prefer the latter."

'That article was written by Mr Heseltine. He is now President of the Board of Trade, but in 1989, when he was a backbencher, he was free to say what he thought. How many Conservative members are there who, given the freedom to do so, would gladly vote for the social chapter tonight? I am genuinely sorry Mr Heseltine cannot take part in this debate. I am sure he represents many other Conservative members who share his point of view.'

It is one of the hazards of political life that your words come back to haunt you. Edwina Currie, pretty and feminine until she opens her mouth when she becomes a virago, was next on her feet. 'Many of us have no problem with the social dimension. It is the detail of the protocol we dislike and wish to vote against,' a rather weak statement, I thought, simply to tell the world and the people she hopes will vote for her next year that she's all for Europe.

Edwina has already announced she wishes to become an MEP and has been adopted for Bedfordshire South. In my opinion she and all our other Euro-hopefuls are going to have their work cut out. I think they'll have a very tough time getting Conservative party supporters to turn out and vote because they are so brassed off with all this Euro-stuff. I very much suspect next year's Euro-election will be the referendum on government policy we are not being allowed to have.

When I made the occasional sortie out of the chamber I saw there was some heavy whipping going on. The atmosphere was nasty. People who had clawed their way to the top could see their careers going down the pan if the Government lost the vote and they were getting vindictive. At one stage seven ministers and a Whip surrounded Iain Duncan-Smith to try to dissuade him from voting with us. Barry Legg was frog-marched to the Chief Whip's office for a dressing-down but they picked the wrong man. He was Shirley Porter's henchman when Lady Porter was leader of Westminster Council and anyone who can handle her can take care of himself. At least, so far tonight, I had been spared. Or so I thought. Suddenly, from the far corner, outside the Labour Whip's office, Nicholas Soames, known by all and sundry as the Butter Mountain from Crawley, came charging across the lobby.

He was carrying, rather awkwardly, one of those over-long bunches of flowers wrapped up in a Cellophane envelope with a huge, unattractive bow. 'I'll give you these, Teresa, if you'll only say you'll vote with the Government,' he said pleadingly.

This must be the first time one member ever offered another a floral tribute before they were dead.

'Wherever did you get them, Nicholas?' I teased him. 'They're horrid. So large and common. I would have given you credit for better taste.'

'I picked them up a few minutes ago in the Labour Whips' office,' he admitted.

'You really will have to get a better florist if you want to woo me,' I told him. 'I've had much better offers than this tonight and, if I may say so, from a better class of minister.'

'Take them,' he pleaded.

'No thanks.'

He got down on one knee as if to propose to me. Then he said, 'Now, will you agree to vote for the Government?'

'Get up! Whatever will people think? Is this a wedding or a funeral bouquet?'

'That depends on you.'

Nicholas is a serious fogey, said to be best chum of the Prince of Wales, who goes huntin' and shootin' at weekends. We are like chalk and cheese and this little charade was absurd.

'Really, Nicholas. Grow up. I don't change my mind that easily.'

'Do you want to humiliate me in front of all the lobby correspondents?' he wailed.

'Yes, I rather think I do. But you may give me a small

peck on the cheek. That will be noted in the diary columns tomorrow.'

'I am quite sure it will,' he said, bending forward reluctantly.

'And now take the flowers back to the Labour party or give them to a member of the Government. They're the ones who are in bed together who presumably enjoy wooing each other with flowers.'

24

THE FLYING
SCOT

Bill Walker, a staunch supporter of Fresh Start, packed his overnight bag. He felt terrible. The mysterious virus infection which had kept him away from the House of Commons for weeks was no better, and it was exacerbated by the back injury sustained in a flying accident many years ago when seven vertebrae were damaged. As he leaned back in the first-class compartment of the Intercity train taking him to London, he thought angrily about the plots his fellow Conservatives had been hatching against him.

First they had tried to remove him from the Scottish backbench committee by moving a vote of no confidence in his chairmanship. 'I wrote to Sir Marcus Fox to complain that it was really out of order,' Bill told me, 'because quite clearly the chairman is elected for a session of Parliament and cannot be removed. Marcus raised it at an open meeting of the 1922 Committee and it was fairly and squarely sat on.'

Then the chairman of the Scottish Conservatives, Lord Sanderson, or Lord Wallpaper as he is known in the party, phoned his association chairman as well as key members of his constituency executive committee, to try to pressure him into voting with the Government in the paving debate.

'I wrote and told them to keep off my patch. We need interference from them like a hole in the head,' said Bill. 'The voters knew exactly what they were getting because at the general election I canvassed on a narrow constitutional platform. I emphasized the huge value to Scotland of our union with the United Kingdom pointing out that in Europe there was a danger it could break up. In fact there are some Scottish Conservatives who want a separate parliament and that's why they are so pro-Europe. During the election I increased my share of the vote.'

During his illness the Scottish Whip Timothy Kirkhope never once got in touch to ask Bill how he was. Yet so fearful were they about the outcome of tonight's debate the Whips had been harassing his family non-stop but were repeatedly informed he was too ill to come to the telephone. Much of the background stirring was carried out by Sir Michael Hirst, a former MP who lost his seat in 1987 and who is President of the Scottish Conservative Association. Could his motive have been to get Bill de-selected and himself handily available to take his place? Perish the thought.

Ian Lang, Secretary of State for Scotland, told Bill, 'You will be on your own if you vote against the Government.' Attacked on all sides, no wonder the poor man was ill. But, if anything, all this orchestrated animosity strengthened his resolve.

We offered to fly a helicopter up to Scotland to bring him down for the mother of all debates but he refused. 'I'll be all right,' he assured us. 'Nothing will stop me getting there.'

Bill hailed a taxi at King's Cross station and gave the address: 'Seventeen Great College Street, Westminster.' It is the house one newspaper dubbed 'Major's House of Horrors', which Bill Cash had turned into a headquarters for his group of helpers. Biddy Cash was waiting to look after him until he could be smuggled into the House of Commons.

Although it is only a short walk under normal circumstances, they were taking no risks and Biddy drove him to the House of Commons and handed him over at St Stephen's entrance to John Wilkinson, who was to take him to the family room. At the very last minute he was going to be escorted to the lobby to vote. He was our secret weapon.

I went for a quick cup of tea and a toasted bacon sandwich. I hadn't eaten all day and this was a good excuse to indulge in something naughty but nice. The tea room was almost empty. I glanced at the clock. It was twenty to ten. The monitor told me David Hunt was on his feet doing the wind-up. I ate quickly, gulped down the last drop of lemon tea and popped the slice of tea-soaked lemon in my mouth. Full of vitamin C, I told myself, as I squeezed it between my tongue and my palate and grimaced as the acid juice ran down my throat. Good for cleaning the breath, and rotting the teeth, I thought, as I hurried to the chamber.

Nick Hawkins, new Conservative member for Blackpool, had one of the last words: 'Does my Right Honourable Friend agree that any member of this House who votes for the social chapter tonight will have to explain to hundreds of his or her constituents why that vote is costing them their jobs? Those members will have that on their conscience for ever,' he pontificated.

Cries of 'Give him a job! Give him a job!' came from the Labour benches.

'I agree with my Honourable Friend,' said David Hunt, who was winding up for the Government. 'The electorate has rejected the Labour party at four successive general elections. The front door to power has been slammed firmly shut on them. No wonder they are slinking round to the back door. It used to be beer and sandwiches at Number

Ten, now they want claret and croissants with the Commission in Brussels,' he cried, with a flourish.

I was always astonished when members of my own party made these remarks. Couldn't they understand that by supporting policies favoured by the Labour party we were courting the threat of more socialist policies to come?

'There is only one place for the United Kingdom to be in the Europe of the next century,' he went on, 'and that is leading from the front.' Some hope. With one vote out of twelve, most of them hungry for more funds from the richer members of the Community, we will be lucky indeed if we don't end up with our pockets turned inside out.

The House procedure required two votes at the end of the debate. Amendments are always taken first, so we would be asked to vote Yes or No on Labour's amendment 'that this House rejects the Government's proposal to omit the social chapter from the Maastricht Treaty'. The second vote is on the main motion, in this case, the Government's proposal to accept Maastricht bar the social chapter. A number of our Fresh Start colleagues, like Rupert Allason, felt unable to vote for the Labour amendment because it would look to the general public as if they supported the social chapter, which most Conservatives are against. We, on the other hand, although we are just as opposed to the social chapter legislation as anyone else, saw it as our opportunity to kill off the Maastricht treaty altogether. We knew the amendment vote would be close. But not as close as it turned out to be.

The division bell rang for the first time and everyone started to move. In another part of the House, John and Bill hurried through Central Lobby where, blocking their path, was one of the Whips, Greg Knight, all six feet three inches of him. 'You are paired,' he said, grabbing at Bill's five feet six. 'You can't vote.'

'I'm not paired,' said Bill. 'That's why I've come all the way down from Scotland.'

'Yes, you are. You'd better come and see your Whip,' Greg ordered.

Bill looked at John and John looked at Greg.

'We have no proof he's paired,' said John, thinking fast on his feet. 'Bill is not fit enough to see the Whip. He's saving his energy to go through the lobby.' And with that they moved away.

Was this encounter a coincidence? How come Greg Knight knew Bill was in London and going to be in the lobby just then? Had there been a spy on the train? Or was there someone at No. 17 who had leaked our secret to a newspaper? We'll probably never know the answer.

Members rushed to get in through the exit door before the doorman closed it off. The two clerks arrived and settled themselves in front of their large sheets of cream paper on which every member of the House is listed.

'I'll cover the Aye lobby to check which of our supporters goes through with the Government,' said Christopher Gill. 'Will you cover the No lobby, Teresa, to see how many of our people vote against? Don't forget to nip through quickly yourself.'

'And you.'

Inside, the space in front of the bar of the House was already packed. No chance of getting in that way. I retraced my steps and entered the No lobby which ran the full length of the House parallel with the chamber. I hurried to the opposite end where the clerks sit during the vote. They were already in place. People whose surnames begin with A to K file through the one on the left, the rest go through the right. I waited for the clerk to arrive, swapping small-talk with one or two Labour members who had already assembled there.

'Going to get it over quickly?' asked one of them, kindly.

'She doesn't want to be seen in here with us riff-raff,' said another.

'You want to swallow the poison quickly,' quipped someone else.

'It isn't easy for a right-winger to vote for the social chapter,' another taunted me.

'I'm voting to dump this wretched Bill. And if your party had any sense they would too. Then your ratings would soar in the country. You might even have a chance of winning an election. It was a bad day for the Labour party when Neil Kinnock did his U-turn,' I bounced back. This was a reference to the fact that, before Neil Kinnock's leadership, the Labour party had officially opposed European union. Some of them still do.

'Teresa Gorman,' I said, poking my finger towards the spot on the page where I knew the Gs were located. He gave a large tick. Others around me were calling their names. We moved past the clerk to stand hard up against the glass doors waiting for the doorman to open them. As soon as the two Whips outside had arrived and taken their places, one each side, the doorman would open the door just enough to allow members out, one at a time.

I stood in the entrance and bowed.

'One,' called Irvine Patnick, the Conservative Whip on duty as I came through. His counterpart opposite nodded, but didn't say anything as is the custom.

Outside, I turned immediately and stood close behind

Irvine and to the side where I could watch members coming through without appearing conspicuous. We watched carefully whether the Ulster Unionists would vote with the Government or, as they had sometimes done in the past, abstain. It soon became obvious they were voting.

I stood behind the charming Mr Patnick, counting people as they came through for the Conservatives. Opposite him Ray Powell was counting for Labour.

I began counting Fresh Start people. Nick Budgen, John Butcher, Bill Cash, James Cran, I quickly jotted down their names on the back of an envelope.

'Ninety-two,' called Irvine Patnick.

'Ninety-three.' Ray Powell nodded.

'Ninety-four.' Again Ray Powell indicated his agreement.

Suddenly Bill Walker appeared in the doorway. He stopped and bowed.

'Paired,' shouted Irvine Patnick.

'Not paired,' shouted Ray Powell.

'Ninety-five.'

'Ninety-four,' shouted Irvine again.

The group of members behind me surged forward surrounding the two tellers. The Labour Chief Whip, Derek Foster, appeared on the other side of the doors. 'Get back,' he yelled at the crowd, who immediately took a step backwards.

'Not paired,' he said firmly.

Andrew Mitchell, a newly appointed Whip, stepped forward to Irvine Patnick's side as if to support him. Two members of the Labour party detached themselves from the group behind me and grabbed him, one on each arm. They pulled him backwards. 'Don't you interfere, you public school twit,' one of them said. I watched Andrew's face. It registered more surprise than fear or anger. He made no attempt to resist them.

Ray Powell's voice rang out again.

'Not paired,' he said firmly.

Irvine Patnick hesitated as if trying to remember the counting.

'Ninety-five,' I said, from behind him.

'Ninety-five,' he repeated.

'Ninety-five,' said Ray Powell.

The counting continued. There was no sign of Bill Walker. Someone had spirited him away during the confusion. By now I had counted through twenty-six of our supporters. It looked promising. The Whips compared notes. A buzz went round the group who had been waiting outside the door with me. They surged towards the chamber as the two tellers tried to fight their way through. I turned away towards the members' lobby. Nick Budgen was there. 'It looks good,' I said. 'I think we've won.'

Behind me, Bob Hughes, another Whip, detached himself from the crowd. 'You ....s,' he said furiously, grabbing at my arm. I elbowed him aside and moved into the members' lobby to get away from him. He pursued me. 'You ....ing little ....,' he yelled again.

'Buzz off,' I said gesturing back towards the chamber. 'That's where you usually shout your abuse.' I could feel my temper rising. It was true: Hughes was often reprimanded by the Speaker for shouting abuse at the Labour benches. In the corridors leading off the empty chamber I could see the lobby correspondents straining their ears, scribbling in their notepads. During a vote they are not allowed inside the lobby.

Nick Budgen came up to me. 'Why don't you go along to the tea room and have a quiet cup of tea?' he suggested, trying to defuse the situation.

'I don't want a cup of tea. I want to be in there when the votes are declared.' I battled my way back in time to hear Betty repeat the result.

The Speaker calmed the House with difficulty. The vote was read out. 'The Ayes to the right, 317, the Noes to the left, 317.' A great cheer went up. When the noise died down, Betty Boothroyd spoke again: 'The numbers being equal, it is my duty to cast my vote. It is not the function of the chair to create a majority on a policy issue where no majority exists amongst the rest of the House. In accordance with precedent I therefore cast my vote with the Noes.'

It took the casting vote of the Speaker to save Major's skin. The chamber, packed for the nail-biting finish, with the results in doubt until the final moments, erupted in an orgy of excitement and fury.

The second vote was more decisive. 'Ayes to the right, 316, Noes to the left 324. So the Noes have it.' A great cry went up from the Labour party. They were on their feet cheering and waving; the Conservatives looked grim. The Government had lost by eight votes.

I had mixed feelings about our victory. It wasn't pleasant to see the Labour party so triumphant but it was the price we had to pay for defeating the treaty.

This was the most dramatic parliamentary event since the fall of the Callaghan government in 1979. John Major had failed to secure the go-ahead to ratify the treaty which he had helped to negotiate and which he had always regarded as his personal triumph.

Twenty-three of us voted against the Government this

time. Some abstained, Rupert Allason went home for the evening.

The decision to table an immediate vote of confidence, backed by the threat of an election, was agreed by the Cabinet in an emergency meeting in John Major's Westminster room. Grim-faced, flanked by the Foreign Secretary, Douglas Hurd, and the Chancellor, Kenneth Clarke, the Prime Minister rose to announce his decision to fight the battle all over again the following morning. His declaration that there was a majority in the Commons for ratifying the treaty but no majority for the social chapter brought shouts of 'No!' from the Labour MPs.

Later that night Downing Street confirmed that if the Government's confidence motion was carried it would go ahead with the treaty; if not, the Prime Minister would tender his resignation and the Government would call a general election.

'Order!' called the Speaker. 'Members must come to order. Honourable Members who are standing at the bar of the House must sit down.' Members who had been crowding into the centre of the chamber melted away. It was impossible even for someone of my size to insinuate themselves anywhere near the front of the mêlée.

The Prime Minister rose. 'As a result of the vote the Maastricht Act cannot come into force. We clearly cannot leave the matter there. It cannot be allowed to fester any longer. I therefore give notice that the Government will invite the House tomorrow to support the Government's policy on the social chapter by tabling a motion of confidence in the following terms: "That the House has confidence in the policy of Her Majesty's Government on the adoption of the protocol on the social policy."'

I turned to Bill Cash who was standing behind me. 'What does that mean?' I asked him.

Ten minutes ago we had won the battle for Maastricht. Now the Prime Minister was moving the goal posts. He was not just asking for a vote of confidence in his government, which all Conservatives would have supported, but was attaching that vote to the adoption of the Government's policy on the social chapter. We were back to square one. If we supported that, the Government had the mandate it needed to ratify the treaty. If we didn't, many of us would probably not be MPs for much longer. I only knew that the Government's strategy was meant to save face: they were clinging to this wretched treaty at any price.

After the Prime Minister's announcement, I made my way back to Central Lobby. It was packed with members of the general public who had come to see the fun. Friends I had met there earlier were still waiting.

'You've heard the result?' I asked Robin Forrest, chairman of my ward when I served as a Westminster councillor. 'I'm sorry I couldn't get you a ticket to the gallery.'

'Never mind. It was nearly as exciting in here, watching the comings and goings. We heard the cheer when the vote was announced.'

Just then Roger Gale, the MP for Thanet North, came past me. He stopped long enough to mutter insults at me to the startled amazement of my group of friends.

'What was all that about?' asked Robin, a look of stunned disbelief on his face.

'Take no notice. He's got a bee in his bonnet. It's not the first time he has attacked me. A lot of members on our side can get pretty nasty over this business. The usual courtesies go out of the window.'

Michael Spicer suffered similar treatment. He was chatting to a group of constituents when Archie Hamilton, the Defence minister, came along. It's quite usual for one member to stop and exchange a greeting with another member's guests, but, to Michael's astonishment, Archie started to berate him for his disloyalty to the Government. Michael was furious. 'I'll remember to pay you the same compliment the next time I see you talking to constituents,' he spat out.

Archie, third son of the Baron Hamilton of Dalwell, looked down his nose from his six feet six inch height. 'I'll look forward to that, old boy,' he said, in a patronizing manner. And added, 'Would be nice, though, if you decided to vote with the Government some time.'

I returned home feeling depressed and miserable to discover that the Whips had been working overtime while we were at the House. There was a ring on the doorbell and Jim opened it to David Amess, Michael Portillo's parliamentary private secretary. David had made himself and Basildon New Town famous, and he is a good friend of ours.

'I answered the doorbell at about half past seven. I thought it was you coming in,' Jim told me. 'He wanted me to impress on you how important it was for you to support the Government. He said it could cause a general election if they lost.'

'And what did you say?' I asked, as I changed into my dressing gown.

'I told him I didn't have any influence on you whatsoever. If I had, we'd probably be living in Portugal, soaking up the sun, drinking wine and going to bed at a respectable hour, not gone midnight.'

I laughed, walked into the bathroom and turned on the shower.

Apparently other colleagues' families had similar experiences. One diligent Whip carried a bottle of 1975 claret to someone else's home in his quest to persuade one of our group – unsuccessfully, but I hope they enjoyed a drink.

Nicholas Winterton was dragged from the chamber to discuss his concerns about the ERM by three Cabinet ministers. Presumably what they told him was enough to win his vote. In any event, he ratted.

'There was some real pork-barrel politics going on tonight,' Tony Marlow said as we walked through the great doors of St Stephen's entrance.

25

LOSER
TAKES ALL

As usual I was an early bird, and more than ready to air my views on the seven o'clock news programmes, the morning after the night before. The area was festooned with radio vans, television cables trailing along the pavements and camera crews, their outdoor microphones covered in grey fur fabric to muffle the noise of the wind. Like groups of anxious chipmunks, journalists peered around looking for the MPs they had arranged to interview.

'The Prime Minister has got the party by the goolies,' I said into the ITV camera. 'We won last night and now he has shifted the goal posts. He's told the referee that if he can't have his way, he will take the ball and leave the field.' I felt angry and deflated.

'But isn't it the truth that the Prime Minister is going to win this morning? Your party can't afford a general election.'

'Not necessarily. There are a number of things we can do. The Fresh Start group will be meeting later to discuss our strategy.'

'But wasn't your cause doomed all along?' asked the reporter, trying to needle me.

'You should ask the public. Or take a look at my postbag. The public don't want this treaty and we will keep fighting against it.'

As I walked towards the spot where BBC breakfast

television had set up its shop with Nicholas Witchell inter-viewing a constant stream of members, I bumped into John Wilkinson. 'It's blackmail. We could call their bluff. They can't afford a general election and they know it. We still have everything to play for. Don't give an inch on television,' he advised.

His words surprised me. I had come to believe that maybe there was little more we could do. 'You'll be at the meeting at ten o'clock?' I said.

'Yes. We're not done for until the last bullet is fired.' If any of our group was to see this thing through to the bitter end, it would be John Wilkinson. I had often admired his single-mindedness. He epitomized the view that you shouldn't go to war if you don't want to win.

I gave an interview to the *Today* programme. Waiting to talk to them after me was Nick Budgen and we stepped away a few paces to be out of their earshot.

'The Prime Minister has us over a barrel,' he said with a shrug of resignation.

'I don't agree. Who has most to lose – us or them?' I said. 'It's vital that we don't just curl up and die. What's this last eighteen months been for?'

Ken Maginnis, the Ulster Unionist member for Ferman-agh and South Tyrone, was waiting to speak to another programme.

'What can you Ulster Unionists possibly have got out of the Prime Minister to make you vote for this treaty last night? You, above all people. You have it in your election manifesto that you would oppose it,' I said to him.

'What we made was a small investment for the future,' he said enigmatically.

'Well, I hope you didn't sell yourself too cheaply. What's bought on Thursday can be sold on Monday,' I said. 'I hope you got something in writing.'

The Ulster Unionists were playing their cards close to their chests. Rumours were flying around about the concessions they had extracted from the Prime Minister. The most likely one, I thought, would be a promise that the Government would not go out of its way to oppose the Ulster Unionist candidates with Conservatives from the embryo Conservative party in Northern Ireland, which I had helped to launch at the last Blackpool conference in spite of opposition from the upper echelons.

On Friday, the debate always starts at nine thirty. Unusually for that hour the chamber was packed.

'Parliament must put the stalemate over Europe behind it. I am not prepared to let it poison the political atmosphere any longer. The boil must be lanced and it must be lanced today,' said the Prime Minister in his opening remarks. 'The motion of confidence before the House today is precisely the one that was defeated yesterday. At the conclusion of today's debate either the Government will have won the vote of confidence or I shall see a dissolution of Parliament.' We listened in silence. The Prime Minister looked grim and determined and he spoke strongly. He was soon quoting the chairman of ICI. Just lately his speeches had been peppered with references to him – so much so that I wondered whether ICI had rented a desk in Sarah Hogg's office. As usual, ICI were telling us that British business could not afford the social chapter. For that matter, I thought, we couldn't afford the £50 million a week we are already paying for the membership of the European Community.

I stood at the side of the House and listened for twenty

minutes, then left the chamber and made my way to room J in the basement. The Prime Minister was still speaking. Michael turned up, then John Wilkinson and one or two others.

'I don't think we're going to get much of a turn-out while the Prime Minister is still on his feet. I suggest we go back to the chamber and reschedule this meeting for when he has finished. Let's say around eleven o'clock. Can you arrange that, Teresa? And can you get a message to the rest of our colleagues?'

'It won't be easy. I saw most of them sitting on the benches before I left the chamber,' I said.

I have spent my life as my own boss, ordering around office staff. Now I know how it feels to be on the receiving end. The others made their way back into the chamber. I stayed behind to scribble a note, copied it twenty-six times, folded each one and named each envelope. Fifteen minutes later I began searching along the benches for Fresh Start people. As discreetly as possible I handed the envelope to the person sitting at the end of the bench where I spotted one of them. He glanced at the name and passed it on, so it made its way along the bench until it reached its destination. Some members, on reading the name on the envelope, looked back at me and paused, as if they did not intend to pass it on. The notes were opened carefully, screened from view, and read quickly.

'Meeting, usual place, as soon as the Prime Minister finishes speaking or by eleven,' it said. The member looked up and gave me an almost imperceptible nod. My discreet activities, meant to attract as little attention as possible, were being filmed by the television cameras and, I learned afterwards, transmitted with a running commentary.

'Teresa Gorman has just entered the chamber and is distributing information to the Fresh Start group.'

Twenty minutes later the commentary began again. 'The Euro-rebels have yet to decide their position. They are rumoured to be meeting again this morning. I have just seen Michael Spicer get up and leave the chamber. And there goes Teresa Gorman . . . Teddy Taylor and Richard Shepherd. Now Ann Winterton is getting to her feet and Bill Cash is on the move. Yes, they are definitely moving out of the chamber to meet somewhere.'

John Smith was speaking as I checked to see if any of our members were still there. Nicholas Winterton was in his usual seat on the front bench below the gangway and seemed engrossed in John Smith's remarks. Listening to a debate is like watching a game of tennis: no matter which side you're on you applaud good shots by the opponent. So it was on Friday. The leader of the Labour party was making a very good speech in which he spelt out the illogicality at the heart of the Prime Minister's argument.

'There was not a hint of the problems that were to come when the Prime Minister advertised his visit to Maastricht as game, set and match. He is saying, nineteen months later, after endless footfaults he is struggling with a tie-break and like some petulant prima donna he is threatening to take his racquet away. He told us how crucial it was to be on the inside track, shaping events, defending Britain's interests. He warned us that if we throw away our capacity to defend our interests this country will pay a heavy price in the years to come.

'What kind of triumph is it that our ace negotiator leaves the court whenever key policies on employment are discussed? We cannot be in Europe and out of it at the same time. That is the fundamental contradiction at the heart of his arguments.'

I had to agree. You cannot have a little of Maastricht any more that you can be a little pregnant.

A number of colleagues had already arrived when I reached the room. The mood was sober in contrast to the jollity of the night before. Michael Spicer was already in his place at the head of the table, scribbling a letter.

'What are you writing Michael, your suicide note?' I asked him.

'No. I'm dropping a line to a close colleague who let us down last night and voted with the Government.' He didn't venture a name and I didn't ask for one.

There was a feeling of restlessness in the room. Edward Leigh was there. But no Rupert Allason.

'What happened to Rupert last night? Did he vote with the Government or abstain?'

'He abstained on both votes.'

'So Christopher says, and he keeps a very close check on these things.'

Several colleagues were clearly unhappy with the presence in the room of people who had apparently changed their minds, not so much because of their actions, although we were bitterly disappointed, but because they had failed to make it clear to their colleagues with whom, for eighteen months, they had shared this fight.

I tapped Michael on the arm as he was finishing his letter. 'I think perhaps you should deal with this. Some people are unhappy about people here who voted with the Government last night. There's a feeling it would be more appropriate if they left. Someone else must have told them about the meeting because I didn't.'

Michael looked up from his letter. 'Who is it?'

Before I could answer Bernard Jenkin spoke. 'I'll leave if you prefer.'

'I think it might be better,' I said. 'People are feeling a little tense.'

Bernard got up. So did Roger Knapman.

In last night's vote several of our supposedly most dedicated colleagues voted with the Government: John Carlisle, Michael Lord, Nicholas Winterton, John Biffen and Bernard Jenkin. But Roger Knapman puzzled me. He had appeared to be one of the most ferocious opponents of Maastricht, voting forty-four times against the Government. He had resigned as a PPS because of Maastricht. He had been one of our whips, our liaison man with the Ulster Unionists. Only ten minutes before the vote last night I had heard him remonstrating with James Cran, urging him to vote with us on the first of last night's amendments, even though James had made it clear at our meeting he would not do so. Yet he then went and voted against our position twice.

'I saw no point in holding out last night,' he said now. 'I took John Biffen's position that the game was already over.'

As Bernard and Roger left I felt a deep sadness. At least they came and faced the music. Other colleagues kept away.

What pressures had they been subjected to? What arguments could change a person's view after many months of battle?

With their departure the tension in the room eased. Michael spoke. 'First, I must congratulate colleagues. But, from my preliminary discussions, I think the consensus is that there is very little more we can do. Of course, we are not being asked to vote on a straight confidence motion but on the very point we voted down last night, confidence in the Government's opt-out policies. The alternative seems to be a general election and I sense that you are not in the mood for that.'

Peter Tapsell spoke. 'I agree. We have done all we reasonably can. History will judge us for our battle and our success and it will judge the Government for its manner of overturning it. In time to come, when we are asked what we did when the country was fighting for its right to govern itself, we will be able to hold our heads up and declare we were on the right side.' He paused.

'I don't think the game is up,' said Dick Body. 'I think there's something else we can still do.'

Earlier, after I had finished broadcasting, I had gone up to the House of Commons clerks' office on the third floor to put my name down on the ten-minute-rule Bill list to stake a claim in the next session of Parliament. Sir Richard Body was in the room, in earnest conversation with one of the clerks.

'What are you up to, Dick?' I asked him.

'I'm just sussing out the possibility that the Government's action this morning is illegal,' he said. 'The confidence motion they have tabled seeks to overturn last night's vote. The clerk, here, agrees with me this could be the subject of a legal challenge: the Government is seeking to overturn the will of the House.'

Instantly, my mood brightened.

'Let's go outside and discuss it,' he said, taking my elbow and steering me out of the room. 'I think we might be able to challenge them in the court.'

I was intrigued. We took one of the elderly lifts, the kind that it takes five minutes to get in and out of. First the metal grille, then the inside door. Step inside and you repeat the whole exercise and the lift chugs slowly down. 'It would have been quicker to walk,' I said.

In the lobby we found several Fresh Starters and he explained his idea briefly. 'You must explain to the group when we have our meeting in the bunker.'

Later, looking round the table, Dick said, 'I have checked this with the clerks and they think we would have a perfect right to ask the court for a stay of execution on this motion because it clearly overturns the Government defeat last night. The court's concern would be that the Government is acting improperly, perhaps illegally. If we went to the High Court and asked for the writ it would probably be granted.'

Everyone listened intently. 'I suggest a number of us get into a couple of taxis and beetle up to the courts in the Strand,' he said. 'We can make the powers that be aware of our actions. I don't think the Government would dare to go to the vote if it knew we were seeking a legal opinion.'

'It would certainly give the Whips the fright of their lives if it was reported back we'd decided to spend the morning at the High Court.'

'The public would not understand. It's a risky strategy,' said Barry Legg.

'I'd be prepared to go along with him. Will other colleagues join in?' said Tony Marlow.

We looked round the table. Several nodded. I counted them. To make the strategy effective and put the wind up the Whips we really needed a dozen people to come with us. There were not enough.

'Another option would be to use Dick's idea as a bargaining point with the Government. Michael could seek a meeting with the Chief Whip to negotiate with him to get some sort of a deal,' said Toby Jessel.

'The most we can hope for is a promise of no recriminations against colleagues. That could be a real threat for some of us with boundary changes coming up,' said James Cran.

'I've already had that threat,' said Bill Cash. 'But I'm damned if I'm going to vote this morning to put a Labour government in.'

'The recriminations will undoubtedly go on in some constituencies unless Norman Fowler does something to prevent it. We could use the High Court card as a bargaining counter to persuade him to send a letter to all the constituencies, telling them to put all this behind us.'

'The Foreign Secretary will be winding up the debate. We could ask for a conciliatory gesture in a peace-making speech. No bitterness or recriminations. Draw a line in the sand. That sort of stuff.'

I sensed there was more support for negotiation than for another challenge to the Government's authority. I wrote a note and passed it to John Wilkinson: 'If ever I am in a real war, I want you for one of my generals. You and I are fighting to win.'

He looked up and smiled. He turned the paper over and scribbled something on the back. 'Ditto', it said.

'Then I will go to see Richard Ryder and negotiate something with him, then report back to the group later in the morning. Say two o'clock?'

'Not in the middle of lunch,' exclaimed Ann Winterton, who had been utterly loyal and courageous throughout these events.

'And I'll find out what's the latest time we could ask for

a writ from the High Court. I'm a bit out of touch with these technical details. But if there's anything to say, I'll get in touch with you, Michael,' said Dick.

'And I will ask Teresa to get all this information round to everybody.'

'I'll leave a message for everyone on the board so long as you all remember to pick it up by two p.m.,' I said.

Once again I was sitting alone, jotting down the note I might need to put on the letter board later. I went along to the copier for the second time that morning and addressed twenty-three envelopes, the number of members who had been in the room: those who had voted with us last night.

The corridor was deserted. As I rounded a corner, Michael Forsyth, a minister and a member of the No Turning Back group, appeared as if by magic.

'Can I have a word with you?' he said, looking serious.

I'd known Michael for several years: we had been on Westminster City Council together and shared the same right-wing views.

'The Government is in a very serious position. The Prime Minister really means to resign if the confidence vote goes against him. I want you to understand that we will be into a general election and we are bound to lose.'

'I know all that – but I think the Prime Minister is bluffing. I suppose they sent you to nobble me.'

He didn't answer but the mere fact that he was standing in this empty corridor talking to me, a place where he had no other possible business, told me that the Government was still uncertain of the outcome of the vote.

'Whatever is the matter with the Prime Minister? Doesn't he understand the whole of our unpopularity is rooted in Europe?'

'You don't have to tell me all that, Teresa. You know where my sympathies lie. But we're talking here about fifteen years in the wilderness if we lose this vote. I'm here to ask you not to do it.'

'We haven't made up our minds yet. We're having another meeting before the vote. We have one or two possibilities up our sleeve.' I knew he would go back and tell the Whips.

'It seems to me we are rapidly moving back into the bad old days of Edward Heath when we thought we could spend our way out of problems. That's not the Conservative party I joined.'

'I know, I know, Teresa, I don't necessarily disagree with you.' The more he talked to me, the more determined I felt. Saying these things out loud somehow strengthened my own resolution.

Michael looked sheepish. 'It's the price you pay for remaining in government.'

I don't know about a funny old world, it's certainly a cynical one. I phoned my office.

'Anything in from the constituency?' I asked, knowing that after the furore of last night's debate there were always messages on the answering machine and faxes from people anxious to pass on their opinions – for or against the stand I had taken.

'We've had several telephone calls from members of the executive, Frank Tomlin and Don Morris, to say well done last night, but don't bring the Government down.'

'Anything else?'

'You've got half a dozen faxes and lots more messages from the public, I should think about forty, all saying much the same thing.'

'What's your assessment of the general mood?' I asked Brian, my research assistant.

'Well, I'd say sixty per cent are from Tories saying spare us a Labour government and forty per cent saying go the whole way.'

26

LUNCH ON THE TERRACE

I thought about what Brian had told me as I made my way back to Central Lobby, where I bumped into Christopher again.

'What are you doing for lunch?' he asked me. 'Shall we have it together?'

'It's a lovely sunny day. Shall we see if there's any room in the terrace dining room?'

'What response are you getting from your constituency?' I asked him. 'Mine's about sixty–forty for supporting the Government today.'

We were about to leave the lobby when Sir Peter Tapsell came through.

'Peter. You must owe me a drink by now after all those letters I've been sending you. Why don't you join us for lunch on the terrace?'

'I'll buy you some champagne. I think the occasion calls for it.'

On the way down to the dining room, we picked up Toby Jessel. I linked arms with Toby and Peter and we were laughing as we walked the length of the terrace to the awning, which covered it at the far end, where lunch was served. Gillian Shepherd, the Minister for Agriculture, looked up, her attention attracted by our noisy joviality. I looked at her: it was the only time I can ever remember seeing her without a smile on her face. We stopped at the terrace bar for a drink. A number of newspaper and television reporters were there. In the corner a couple of Europhiles sipped drinks and nibbled peanuts. 'Have you given up?' one of them called.

'No fear,' I said.

'You haven't any shots left in your rifle.'

'Not true. Can't you see we're all smiling?'

'Can John Major survive as prime minister?' asked a reporter. It was the topic of the day.

'He's bound to win the vote today.'

'Unless we have it stopped.'

'What do you mean?' they said, all agog.

'Well, they could decide to withdraw the motion, couldn't they?' I said teasingly.

The reporter furrowed his brow, trying to work out what we meant. 'Tell me more.'

'No time.'

'We'd better go and claim our table,' said Christopher. As we walked in, heads turned. Every table in the dining room is hosted by at least one MP. Guests looked over their shoulders like a lot of ducks about to clean their wings with their beaks as they were told, 'There go the people who voted against the Government last night.'

'I'm ordering the champagne, and I want it in a jug,' said Peter Tapsell to the wine waiter.

'And this is a buffet lunch room and we have to go up and choose our lunch,' I said.

On my way back to the table, I spotted Tony Newton, the Leader of the House, lunching with his wife Patricia. I recently bought a house in my constituency from her: she is a negotiator for a property company. Tony looked pale and drawn.

'Patricia, I couldn't pass by without having a word. I'm not quite sure whether Tony is still speaking to me after last night,' I said.

'I don't think he's been to bed for a week,' she said.

'Of course, Teresa, I'm still talking to you. We must keep up civilized standards of behaviour even if some of us sometimes go off the rails,' he said with a smile.

'How's business? Have you sold any nice houses lately?' I asked Patricia.

'Not bad. Some interesting properties like the one you've just bought are selling. They're one-offs and there's always a market for them.'

'That's a relief,' I said. 'If there are any recriminations and I get de-selected we might come back to you to sell it for us again.'

'Not much chance of that,' said Tony. 'Your seat is pretty safe in the boundary reshuffle, isn't it?'

Tony and I are both Essex MPs and keenly interested in the Boundary Commission's proposals to mess about with our constituencies. Tony's is particularly affected.

'Keep our fingers crossed and hope that we don't have a general election on our hands in the near future,' I joked.

'That's up to you,' he said, with mock severity. 'You'd better make sure you're in the right lobby this afternoon.'

Walter Sweeney soon joined our tiny table for four and he perched at one corner.

'I'll get the next course,' said Sir Peter. 'Anything you fancy?'

'You choose.'

Before he returned, Michael Spicer arrived.

'Shall I get you something to eat before you begin dishing the dirt?' I asked him.

'No, I'll get it. I haven't got very long. I'm having another meeting in half an hour's time.'

Michael told us he had seen Richard Ryder. They had been joined by Douglas Hurd. They had discussed possible statements to defuse things between the rebels and the Government.

Michael had told them what he thought the Fresh Start group would consider a conciliatory gesture. 'Richard's position is that we had an honourable battle and our views would be respected in future discussions on European legislation. There would be no attempt to railroad through anything like this again,' he said. 'I formed the opinion that the Government is exhausted and still extremely nervous. He recognizes that the man in the street is on our side and that our moral position is stronger than the Government's.'

'Did he say that?'

'Well, not quite. That's just my interpretation. I think his heart is with us even if his head isn't.'

'And will there be any references in his speech to foreign policy and defence?' asked Walter Sweeney.

'Well, I put all our points to the Foreign Secretary. It's up to him to go away and decide what he's going to say. I hope he makes enough concessions for all of our group to vote with the Government. I don't fancy spending the rest of the day at the law courts. I want to get back to the constituency.'

We laughed. Although I would have relished the spectacle of us all piling into taxis in the next half-hour, to the consternation of the Whips, I could see our chances of pulling it off slipping away.

In spite of the anger and frustration we felt at being so

near to killing off the treaty and (perhaps?) altering the whole of our constitution, we had the satisfaction of knowing we had won a moral victory. We had shown that a small group of determined MPs prepared to stick to their principles through thick and thin can, almost, move mountains.

We also had the satisfaction of knowing that many government ministers were secretly on our side and that they were scared out of their wits about what we might do this afternoon.

Normally considered such important people, far too busy and godlike to bother with we lowly mortals, this Friday morning they had been detailed to search us all out and have 'words'. We had all been approached by someone from the upper echelons, pressing us at this eleventh hour not to vote against the confidence motion. They were sent out like ferrets to chase rabbits. They knew we had them over a barrel and that their jobs were on the line; there'd hardly be any of them left if we had a general election. It was estimated we could lose by as many as 180 seats and all of us had had frantic phone calls from our constituency associations to say, 'Enough is enough.'

It was a power we enjoyed wielding and I suggested mischievously, 'Why don't we all hop into taxis and go to Victoria? We can spend the day at the seaside in Brighton.' Round the table we all agreed – but we would have to muster the numbers to make it a feasible option. Frustratingly, we couldn't.

'What about recriminations?' asked Walter, who had been paying close attention to Michael's description of the meeting.

'I'm going back in ten minutes for another meeting with

Richard and Norman Fowler. I'm going to ask him to write a letter to all constituency chairmen to tell them that there's to be no back-biting, no de-selections, we want a line drawn in the sand under the whole episode.'

27

THE END OF
THE AFFAIR

The debate was still churning on while we were having our jolly lunch but there was no one we felt like leaping up to listen to. Now it was nearly two thirty and as we strolled back in, who should be on his feet but my favourite speaker. Ted Heath was in full flow, praising the Prime Minister for the umpteenth time.

'My Right Honourable Friend has acted with complete honesty and great integrity. For that he is to be loudly and widely commended.'

The chamber was fairly empty. Sitting opposite him was Dennis Skinner, who spends more time in there than anyone, chipping in provocative comments whenever he can.

'There is obviously an enormous amount to be done to inform people about the Maastricht treaty and the work of the European Community and its commissioners,' Heath droned.

'What for? Nobody wants it,' shouted Dennis.

'I know the Honourable Gentleman does not like it but, thank God, his view is not characteristic of the British people. We hear talk about democracy but it is not democracy if a small group defies and brings to nothing the major decisions taken by the House at the second and third reading of a Bill.

'They talk of principles. How can it be principled to vote with the Opposition in favour of something which, on principle, you are absolutely opposed to?' he said referring to last night's vote.

'I have been a member of the Conservative party for almost sixty years, through good times and bad times, in government and out of government. I do not want it brought to an end by a small minority in our parliamentary party.'

I'd heard enough. Anyway, there was a meeting scheduled for three in our little bunker. Michael was already there, prepared, as always, to steer us through our last move.

'The Government has overplayed its hand on the vote of confidence card. This is the second time he has done it. How many times can a prime minister threaten to resign and still be believed?'

'You mean, before someone takes him up on his offer?' We laughed.

'He can't pull this one again for a long time,' he said. 'In 1996 at the next European conference we can fight again, roll something back of the powers they are giving away. We have established excellent contacts with politicians in other European countries who feel as we do. The tide is with us. We have only to come together again to generate fear in the Cabinet. As for Richard Body's suggestion of calling the Government's bluff, there was not enough support among members to take it further.'

I felt sad as we returned to the chamber. Douglas Hurd was winding up the debate. 'This is the last speech of the last debate on the ratification of the Maastricht treaty,' he began.

'Hear, hear!' shouted some members.

I listened carefully for the conciliatory remarks he had promised to Michael Spicer.

'I have often wished them to go away, go to bed, get

lost. However, I do not doubt that their struggle and arguments will find a remembered place in the annals of parliamentary conflict.'

This was conciliation?

He went on, 'I would not like to end this debate without saying a warm thanks to those who, throughout everything, supported the Government's side. They have worked morning, noon and night to safeguard our place in Europe. They have gained less publicity than the others but without their help we would not have reached this point and we would not have prevailed.'

He heaped praise on Ted Heath three times and I looked round for Michael Spicer to see what his reaction was. We both pulled a face. Apart from Tam Dalyell, no one sought to intervene in the Foreign Secretary's summing up. Mr Delors came in for special praise for his 'fascinating analysis'. So, too, did Tom King, Sir Peter Emery and Paul Channon, all dedicated pro-Europeans.

'The good economic news is actually flowing in faster than either the Chancellor or the Government expected. The political mood of the country often starts in this House. It takes time to spread outward and percolate down to the people.'

Yes, he would think that, but that is what is wrong with this Cabinet, I thought. Politics should not come from the top downwards but from the grass roots upwards.

'I believe that under the leadership of the Prime Minister we have cultivated the land well despite much rough weather. I believe we have sown good seeds and that we can now work together to bring in a good harvest.'

At four thirty John Major won his vote of confidence.

Every Conservative MP, with the well-documented exception of Rupert Allason, voted with the Government. The Speaker declared the result: a majority of thirty-nine.

As he left the chamber the Prime Minister put his arm around Ted Heath's shoulder before making an unusual departure through the grand entrance of the members' lobby, rather than his usual exit behind the Speaker's chair.

I stayed behind for a while to ponder on our future.

This ridiculous treaty would do so much damage to the country and to the party.

If only politicians would leave people alone, they will respond. Our preoccupation with Europe is a weakness, not a strength.

If only Brussels wouldn't meddle with business, business would create the jobs people need.

There are fifty to one hundred Conservative MPs who believe in free trade, most of them are businessmen and women so they understand the pressures of industry and the market. We are a large and potentially influential block if we can get our act together. But free trade is not a panacea. We need to stick to our promise of lower taxes and stop government from meddling with the currency. That would guarantee a stable pound and low interest rates.

Above all, we need someone who believes in governing the country from Britain not Brussels.

I sighed and made my way out of a now silent and empty chamber. We shall fight on, but isn't it unbelievable that we have to fight our own side – the party who should know this off by heart?

28

THE BASTARDS

The Prime Minister had just finished a television interview with Michael Brunson, ITN's political editor. They were reviewing the confidence vote.

The camera lights were switched off, the Prime Minister leaned back in his chair, unclipped a small microphone from beneath his tie and said in a jocular tone, 'What I don't understand, Michael, is why such a complete wimp like me keeps winning everything. The way people who oppose our European policy go about it is to attack me personally. Think of it through my perspective. You have three right-wing members of the Cabinet. What happens if they resign? Where do you think most of the poison has come from? It's coming from the dispossessed and the never possessed on the back benches. Would you like three more of the bastards out there? What's the Lyndon Johnson maxim?'

'If you've got them by the balls, their hearts and minds will follow,' said Brunson chuckling.

'No, that's not what I had in mind – though it's pretty good.'

POSTSCRIPT

MAJOR BACKS PURGE OF TORY RIGHT
LOYALISTS PLAN REVENGE ON REBEL MPS

John Major has given his approval for a 'revenge attack' on Conservative MPs who have rebelled against his government and have spoken out against his style of leadership. Back-benchers on the left of the party have told him they plan an offensive against the right to capture the backbench committee posts. Senior party sources confirmed last night that Major has taken an active interest in their plan and has discussed strategy.

George Gardiner said last night, 'I know I am a prime target particularly for the Euro-fanatics.'

Sunday Times, 22 August 1993

THE ROAD TO RUIN

John Major will be making a catastrophic blunder if he takes revenge against his Tory critics.

A report in the *Sunday Times* says he is planning a purge to force them out of key committees in the Commons.

Does he have a death wish?

The awkward-squad was RIGHT to fight Maastricht. RIGHT to demand cuts in state spending. RIGHT to resist tax increases.

The 'trouble-makers' represent the Tory heart and soul.

And if John Major gets rid of them, the voters will exact a terrible revenge of their own.

Sun, 23 August 1993

THE TORY REBEL LEAGUE

R = Rebellion: a vote against the Government.   A = No vote.
G = voted with the Government.   * shows a member of the 1992 intake.

		R	A	G	Pts
Cash, W	Stafford	47	13	2	107
Winterton, N	Macclesfield	46	15	1	107
Taylor, Sir T	Southend E	48	10	4	106
Winterton, Mrs A	Congleton	44	17	1	105
*Knapman, R	Stroud	44	16	2	104
Gill, C	Ludlow	43	17	2	103
Skeet, Sir T	Beds N	41	19	2	101
Jessel, T	Twickenham	42	16	4	100
Gorman, Mrs T	Billericay	40	19	3	99
Walker, B	Tayside N	39	19	4	97
Lawrence, Sir I	Burton	38	21	3	97
Spicer M	Worcs S	37	23	2	97
Marlow, T	Northampton N	36	25	1	97
Budgen, N	Wolverhampton SE	36	24	2	96
Shepherd, R	Aldridge	34	26	2	94
Lord, M	Suffolk Central	35	23	4	93
Cran, J	Beverley	30	31	1	91
Wilkinson, J	Ruislip	31	28	3	90
Body, Sir R	Holland	30	28	4	88
Biffen, J	Shropshire N	26	35	1	87
Tapsell, Sir P	Lindsey E	24	34	4	82
Carlisle, J	Luton N	21	40	1	82
Butcher, J	Coventry SW	19	43	0	81
Gardiner, Sir G	Reigate	23	34	5	80
Hawksley, W	Stourbridge	18	44	0	80
*Sweeney, W	Vale of Glam	21	36	5	78
*Legg, B	Milton Keynes SW	18	41	3	77
Carttiss, M	Gt Yarmouth	17	41	4	75
Porter, D	Waveney	15	44	3	74
Allason, R	Torbay	12	46	4	70
Duncan-Smith, I	Chingford	11	47	4	69
Bendall, V	Ilford N	4	56	2	64
Boyson, Sir R	Brent N	12	39	11	63
Pawsey, J	Rugby	14	34	14	62
Townend, J	Bridlington	6	50	6	62
Moate, Sir R	Faversham	4	53	5	61
Bonsor, Sir N	Upminster	3	55	4	61
*Jenkin, B	Colchester N	1	58	3	60
Baker, K	Mole Valley	1	56	5	58
Fry, P	Wellingborough	5	47	10	57
Clark, Dr M	Rochford	2	51	9	55
*Whittingdale, J	Colchester S	1	41	20	43
Hunter, A	Basingstoke	5	24	33	34
Vaughan, Sir G	Reading E	1	27	34	29
Walden, G	Buckingham	0	24	38	24
Grylls, Sir M	Surrey NW	0	17	45	17
Greenway, H	Ealing N	4	8	50	16